Charming Colorwork Socks

25 Delightful Knitting Patterns for Colorful, Comfy Footwear

Charlotte Stone

Creator of Stone Knits

PAGE STREET
PUBLISHING CO.

PAGE STREET
PUBLISHING CO.

First published in 2022 by
Page Street Publishing Co.
27 Congress Street, Suite 1511
Salem, MA 01970
www.pagestreetpublishing.com

Distributed by Macmillan, sales in Canada by The Canadian Manda Group.

26   25   24   23   22   2   3   4   5

ISBN-13: 978-1-64567-680-5
ISBN-10: 1-64567-680-3

Library of Congress Control Number: 2022935241

Cover and book design by Molly Kate Young for Page Street Publishing Co.
Photography by Charlotte Stone

Printed and bound in the United States

For Alex, Betsy, Lola and Zak
(who continuously inspire me to knit more socks)

Table of Contents

Introduction   7

Knitting Colorwork Socks:
My Tips and Tricks   8

   Why Colorwork Socks?   8

   Sizing Matters   8

   Gauge for Perfect-Fitting Socks   9

   Floats   10

   Choosing Colors   10

   Color Dominance Explained   11

   Finishing, Blocking and
   Care of Socks   11

Crafty Animals   13

Autumn Mice   15

Dog Walk   19

Counting Sheep   25

Flutterby Butterfly   30

Swan Lake   39

Flower Power   45

Blooming Lavender   47

Forget-Me-Knot   51

Happy Poppy   57

Raindrops on Roses   64

Tiptoe Through the Tulips   71

Food, Glorious Food   77

Cherry on Top   79

Coffee Break   84

Gelato Socks   89

Spicy Socks   94

Vitamin C Socks   101

The Great Outdoors   107

Summer Meadows   109

Forest Walk   113

Grape Picking   119

Midnight in Zermatt   123

Starry Night   129

Celebrate Good Times   135

Christmas Eve Skies   137

Eggs for Easter   144

I Heart Socks   151

I'm Batty for Halloween   155

The Holly and the Ivy   161

Yarn Suppliers   167

Abbreviations   169

Special Techniques   170

Acknowledgments   172

About the Author   173

Index   174

Introduction

I am very excited to welcome you to my first-ever colorwork sock collection. I have had a lot of fun letting my imagination run wild, creating 25 unique and vibrant sock designs for you to knit. Since I started releasing colorwork sock patterns in 2017, I have tried to keep very much within my Stone Knits socks style that you might already know and love. I have been inspired by the nature and culture where I live, here in the hills above Zürich in Switzerland.

I have always had cold feet, so my love of sock knitting started many years ago out of a desire to keep my toes warm. After moving from London to Switzerland with my family, I was suddenly faced with five pairs of feet to keep warm and knit for in the winter. And as I am guessing you already know, once you start wearing hand-knit socks, it is hard to go back to plain shop-bought! Cold feet, coupled with an absolute love for and obsession with knitting colorwork, led me to designing colorwork socks.

I love how, with colorwork socks, we can be so creative with the colors and motifs just by knitting with a couple of colors in one row. The number of designs and colors that can be played with in these patterns is really unlimited. You can use the yarn like you are drawing or painting, and it's so fun to be wild and creative with what you are making, even with such a practical clothing item as socks! With socks, you can go totally out of your comfort zone without being too worried about whether they suit you or if they will go well with your wardrobe!

It is liberating to just choose an outlandish pair of socks for the mood you are in or for celebrating an event or time of the year! Making a Christmas sweater can be a big commitment of yarn, money and time, but I think most of us could happily knit and wear a festive pair of socks (while keeping our feet warm in the winter). Colorwork socks are also a perfect knit to gift, since they are relatively quick to make and will often use up your scrap leftovers of yarn. And seriously, who doesn't need socks!? It's like gifting a hug for the feet! With these patterns you're able to create a thoughtful and personalized pair for your loved ones; for instance, chickens for your chicken-owning friends or Coffee Break (page 84) socks for any coffee addicts you might know. I have created a variety of different designs so that you can find a pattern for everyone!

Go grab your favorite pair of sock needles and rummage through your sock yarn to see which pair you might cast on first! No matter which pattern you choose, you are in for a knitting treat!

Best wishes and happy sock knitting.

Charlotte xx

Knitting Colorwork Socks: My Tips and Tricks

Why Colorwork Socks?

I truly believe there is no "best way" for knitting colorwork. I think the best way to knit colorwork socks is with a smile on your face and an optimistic attitude. Do whatever feels best for you and brings you joy, or whatever you are happy to do for your colorwork technique. Your knitting should be fun and make you happy. You will do more of it if you enjoy the process of knitting your socks.

I am an English thrower–style knitter (holding the yarn in my right hand), and I can knit colorwork socks quickly by picking up and putting down each strand as it is required within the pattern. It is also possible to hold both yarns with your left hand if you are a continental-style knitter. And there are many different yarn holding devices that can help prevent your yarns from twisting. As an alternative, it is totally okay to stop now and then while you are working to untwist any yarn strands so you do not get in a tangle! Another method is to hold one strand of color in one hand and the other color in the other hand. The only problem that I have found with this method is that since one of those ways of knitting feels less familiar, it often results in unequal tension for each color. But as with everything in knitting, this will improve with practice.

Sizing Matters

I really want you to make pairs of colorwork socks that will fit! Every pattern has been written with different stitch counts and size options, to try and ensure everyone is able to wear these socks.

With these colorwork sock patterns, the most important measurement is the circumference of your foot, not the length. We may have small, wide feet or long, thin feet. With all these patterns, you can increase or decrease the length of the leg or the foot to meet the requirements of the foot you are making the sock for. Each pattern will describe how to do this. You will need to measure around the largest part of the foot to get your correct circumference size. This typically would be the ball of the foot, near your toes.

You will see in each pattern there are two measurements: The first is the size foot the sock is intended to fit, and the second is the actual measurement the stitches will create.

You will want to choose from the first set of measurements for your feet. The reason there is a difference is that your sock should have about 1 inch (2.5 cm) of negative ease so they fit snugly on your foot (and do not fall down inside your shoe!).

If you are knitting these socks as a gift, you will need to know the widest circumference of the person's foot (to choose which size to knit) as well as their foot length. I have provided a table showing the standard shoe size foot-length measurements, which will help you determine how long you need to knit the foot of the sock. If you are knitting the socks for yourself, you can always try them on (be careful with your knitting needles though!) to check if they are the right length.

Standard shoe size charts for length of foot

KIDS' SIZES				
US Sizes	EU Sizes	UK Sizes	Inches	CM
10.5	27	9.5	6.625	16.8
11	28	10	6.75	17.1
11.5	29	10.5	7	17.8
12	30	11	7.125	18.1
12.5	30	11.5	7.25	18.4
13	31	12	7.5	19.1
13.5	31	12.5	7.625	19.4
1	32	13	7.75	19.7
1.5	33	14	8	20.3
2	33	1	8.125	20.6
2.5	34	1.5	8.25	21
3	34	2	8.5	21.6
3.5	35	2.5	8.625	21.9
4	36	3	8.75	22.2
4.5	36	3.5	9	22.9
5	37	4	9.125	23.2
5.5	37	4.5	9.25	23.5
6	38	5	9.5	24.1
6.5	38	5.5	9.625	24.4
7	39	6	9.75	24.8

WOMEN'S SIZES				
US Sizes	EU Sizes	UK Sizes	Inches	CM
4	35	2	8.1875	20.8
4.5	35	2.5	8.375	21.3
5	35–36	3	8.5	21.6
5.5	36	3.5	8.75	22.2
6	36–37	4	8.875	22.5
6.5	37	4.5	9.063	23
7	37–38	5	9.25	23.5
7.5	38	5.5	9.375	23.8
8	38–39	6	9.5	24.1
8.5	39	6.5	9.688	24.6
9	39–40	7	9.875	25.1
9.5	40	7.5	10	25.4
10	40–41	8	10.188	25.9
10.5	41	8.5	10.313	26.2
11	41–42	9	10.5	26.7
11.5	42	9.5	10.688	27.1
12	42–43	10	10.875	27.6

MEN'S SIZES				
US Sizes	EU Sizes	UK Sizes	Inches	CM
6	39	5.5	9.25	23.5
6.5	39	6	9.5	24.1
7	40	6.5	9.625	24.4
7.5	40–41	7	9.75	24.8
8	41	7.5	9.938	25.4
8.5	41–42	8	10.125	25.7
9	42	8.5	10.25	26
9.5	42–43	9	10.438	26.7
10	43	9.5	10.573	27
10.5	43–44	10	10.75	27.3
11	44	10.5	10.938	27.9
11.5	44–45	11	11.125	28.3
12	45	11.5	11.25	28.6
12.5	46	12.5	11.563	28.4
13	47	13.5	11.875	30.2
13.5	48	14.5	12.188	31
14	49	15.5	12.5	31.8

Gauge for Perfect-Fitting Socks

You probably already know that gauge is important for successful knitting, but it is even more so for colorwork socks, especially when it comes to the colorwork sections. You will see that for every pattern in this book, the number of stitches for the colorwork are increased in comparison to the plain stockinette sections of the socks. This is to try and prevent the problem of inelastic floats. Those extra stitches will make up for the sock fabric not being as stretchy in colorwork as they would be if you had knitted it in one color. The patterns will always have instructions to decrease the stitches or go back down a needle size for any stockinette sections after the colorwork.

Depending on the stitch count, I will often recommend going up a needle size (increasing gauge) for the colorwork sections to increase the stretchiness of the colorwork knitting. If necessary, you can even go up a further needle size if you find the sock is still not fitting your foot. Likewise, go down a needle size if you find it is too big. If possible, do try your sock on while knitting, to see if it will fit.

For those who are not practiced in measuring gauge, here is a quick overview. Gauge is measured as the number of stitches in 4 inches (10 cm) in the stitch pattern that you are knitting. You can easily make a small swatch with the yarn and needles you wish to use to check if your gauge is the same. If you have more stitches than required in 4 inches (10 cm), your stitches are too small and you need to go up a needle size. If you have fewer stitches than needed in the gauge, your stitches are too big and you should go down a needle size.

Floats

Floats are the strands that are on the wrong side of your work when the color is not being used. Relax and knit those floats loosely. Stop and gently space the stitches out momentarily as you are knitting the colorwork to ensure the tension and the floats are not too tight. It is very important to keep floats nice and loose to prevent the fabric becoming too tight. You do not want your floats to be straight lines from one section to another. You want them to be slightly looped so the threads can stretch when you pull that sock over the heel. I promise you will not get your toes caught in the loops, and after wearing the socks over time, the threads will start to slightly felt themselves together.

Some motifs will have longer floats between the different colors. People often say to literally twist the strands of yarn at the back to trap or catch a long float to avoid fingers or toes being caught in them. I insist you do not twist your floats too often with colorwork socks. I suggest twisting (or trapping) your floats no more often than every seven stitches, and do not twist them tightly. If you are happy carrying your floats for longer than this, then please do so! I have a very fussy (but adorable!) son and I can honestly say he has not once gotten his little toes caught in a float. The knitted stitches for socks are normally much smaller in comparison to a colorwork sweater or even a hat, and so seven stitches will make a strand of thread that is not a great length at all. I have found, however, that if you twist your threads more often with a colorwork sock, there will be more issues with stretching your sock over your heel while putting it on. I try to avoid rules in knitting, but I have learned from this annoying mistake many times!

Also, do not twist your floats near the edge of where your needles join. Let those floats hang loosely there so they can also stretch when the sock is put on.

Do avoid twisting floats in the exact same place on consecutive rounds as this may cause a slight bump or gap at the front of your work.

And finally! If you find you have problems after you have knitted your sock, blocking your knitting afterwards can sometimes help rectify any issues you

may have with tight floats or unevenly knit colorwork. A wet block and gentle use will also help any long floats slightly felt together into the fabric, so toes are much less likely to snag the fabric.

Choosing Colors

Please choose whatever colors you love for knitting your socks. I recommend using colors that contrast so you can clearly see the colorwork pattern that you have knitted. An easy way to see if your colors have enough contrast is to take a photo of the yarns you would like to use together and change the settings to convert the photo into a black-and-white picture (by removing all the saturation/color). Then you can see how strong the contrast is in the black-and-white picture of your yarn. This will confirm whether the colors are contrasted enough.

I also recommend you knit a little swatch so you can see if the colors work well together. This way you will also be able to see if you have the correct gauge for the pattern, which is essential for fit! Sometimes yarns might look great in their skeins next to one another, but once they are knitted together, they might look totally different. A swatch will show you this before you start your socks (and will possibly save you time in the long run!). It is also fun to knit a motif or two in the round as practice, and then use that swatch as a little wrist warmer or even a cup holder.

Color Dominance Explained

With colorwork, you will want the motif you are knitting to really "pop" from the background color. Regardless of your method of knitting (whether continental, English style or using both hands), when knitting stranded colorwork with two or more colors, it is very important to be aware of which strand of yarn is going under the other strand.

The color on the right side will always be going under the other yarn and be more prominent, while the color on the left side will recede to the background. This is because the yarn held lower is dipping down before stranding across to reach the next stitch. The little bit of extra yarn used to do this will make the stitch in the lower yarn just very slightly bigger and therefore stand out more! With the pattern color that is knitting the motif (the contrast color), the yarn thread at the back of your work should always travel under the background color. This way the pattern color will be the dominant color and will really stand out.

I always advise keeping the yarn which you are using for knitting the contrast color on the right side of your knitting and your background color (normally the main color) on your left side. You can even position your yarns on either side of you like this while you are knitting, whether on the sofa, your favorite chair, in bed or while waiting in the car! If you forget to do this, it is not a big problem; the pattern will still show, but the background color will stand out more prominently and hide the motif a little. If at all possible, I recommend positioning your yarn so your pattern motif will really stand out.

Finishing, Blocking and Care of Socks

Sewing in Ends

I will tell you a secret: I hate sewing in ends. My kids have often said to me when they put their socks on, "Ew, Mum, these socks have spaghetti inside them!" For the comfort of your feet and to ensure stitches do not fall out of place, *don't* be like me and *do* sew in the ends of your yarn. There are even methods for weaving in the ends of your yarn as you knit for anyone who might be as lazy as me.

Blocking

Gently washing your socks in cool water with a little bit of wool wash and then laying them flat (or "blocking") will really help even out your stitches and make a smoother-looking fabric. You will be amazed at how blocking colorwork socks will smooth out any uneven stitches or puckering. You really do not need the wooden sock blockers that we often see on the internet (though they do look lovely!). And even just washing and then laying the sock out flat to dry will help your stitches come together. I have even seen people block their socks on bottles with success, too!

Sock Washing and Care

Did you know that hand-knit wool socks do not need washing as often as the shop-bought acrylic ones? You can actually wear wool for days without washing it. Odor-causing bacteria are literally absorbed by wool. Personally, I prefer using wool for my hand-knit socks, but you can use any type of yarn you prefer and that is available to you.

When you do need to wash your socks, you can hand-wash them or machine-wash them on a gentle, cool, wool cycle with wool wash. I recommend following the washing and care instructions normally found on the yarn ball band. The first few times I wash my socks, I will typically hand-wash them to avoid the color from the yarn running. Another tip to prevent this is to use cool water and a small splash of vinegar. Ask me how I know!

My top tip for your hand-knit socks is to always store them away washed and dried in an air-tight bag. Preferably not in a dark place. Dirty socks discarded under the bed (I have two teenagers and a preteen!) are every moth's dream. Again, ask me how I know. . . . (Which leads me to . . .)

Mending

Do mend or darn your socks if holes appear. There are many sewing techniques for repairing holes and worn areas using your needle and thread. You can even knit a different colored patch on them or totally cut off and reknit a worn-out toe.

Crafty Animals

I am a fan of most creatures and love knitting socks dedicated to my favorite animals. Whether you appreciate beautiful butterflies dancing across the meadows or graceful swans floating elegantly across the water. I am certain you will find a pair of socks here to suit your style. Who can resist making a pair of socks to walk their dog with? Or footwear dedicated to the sheep that provide us with wool for our favorite hobby? It is my hope that you will find the perfect pattern in this chapter for yourself or for any other animal lover in your life!

Autumn Mice

For my family, the end of summer and the return to school is always accompanied by a blackberry picking session in the woods. These socks are inspired by these happy memories and the wild bramble bushes with little mice living among their branches, enjoying the blackberry fruits (or so my cat tells me!). I hope these little knitted critters will brighten your day and herald the coming of autumn, the favorite (and perhaps busiest) season for many of us knitters!

Construction Notes

Knit from the top down with a twisted ribbed cuff and a small lace decoration, this sock includes a mouse and brambles colorwork pattern on the leg with some fun blackberry fruit bobbles too. These socks are knit with an eye of partridge heel flap and gusset. They also have a very simple ribbed lace pattern running down the sock to the toe.

Sizing

1 (2, 3)

To fit (foot circumference): 7½ (8½, 9½) inches / 18–20 (20.5–23, 23.5–25) cm

Finished circumference: 6½ (7½, 8½) inches / 15.5–17.5 (18–20, 20.5–23) cm

Recommended ease: Approximately 1 inch / 2.5 cm of negative ease.

Leg/foot length can be easily adjusted. See instructions for details.

Sample shown is knit in size 2 for shoe size US 8.5 (EU 39, UK 6), foot circumference 8¾ inches (22.5 cm).

Materials

Yarn

Fingering weight, GigglingGecko Socklandia Soxs yarn (80% superwash merino wool, 20% nylon), 398 yds (365 m) per 100-g skein

Shown in

MC: Eggplant (1 skein)

CC1: Dusty Rose (1 skein)

CC2: Butterscotch (1 skein)

Any fingering-weight sock yarn can be used for this sock pattern as long as you can obtain the same gauge. A good substitute would be Hue Loco, LolaBean Yarn Co. or any hand-dyed yarn from an indie dyer near you.

Needles

For ribbing, heel, lace pattern, toe and colorwork for size 3: US 1 (2.25 mm), 32-inch (80-cm) circular for magic loop, or DPNs, or two circulars or a 9-inch (23-cm) circular needle (as preferred).

For colorwork for sizes 1 and 2: US 1.5 (2.5 mm), 32-inch (80-cm) circular for magic loop, or DPNs, or two circulars or a 9-inch (23-cm) circular needle (as preferred).

Use size required to obtain gauge.

Important note: *Do check your gauge for fit. Additional sizes can be achieved by going up or down needle sizes.*

Notions

Stitch marker

Scissors

Tapestry needle

(continued)

Gauge

34 sts x 36 rnds = 4 inches (10 cm) for colorwork for sizes 1 and 2.

36 sts x 38 rnds = 4 inches (10 cm) for colorwork for size 3.

32 sts x 42 rnds = 4 inches (10 cm) for all sizes stockinette and ribbing.

Special Techniques

Making Bobbles (Smaller Version) (page 171)

Knitting Colorwork Socks (page 8)

Kitchener Stitch (page 170)

For all abbreviations, see page 169

Autumn Mice Pattern

Cuff

Cast on 56 (64, 72) sts with MC and US 1 (2.25 mm) needle. Divide sts evenly over the two needles and place a marker at the beginning of the round. For

DPNs, place half of your sts on one needle and divide the other half over two needles. PM for BOR. Join to work in the rnd being careful not to twist sts.

Ribbing Rnd: *K1tbl, P1; repeat from * to end of rnd.

Work Ribbing Rnd for a total of 10 rows (approximately 1 inch [2.5 cm]).

Rnd 1: Purl all sts.

Rnd 2: Knit all sts.

Rnd 3: *K2tog, yo; rep from * to the end of the rnd.

Rnd 4: Knit all sts.

Rnd 5: Purl all sts.

Leg

Knit 1 rnd with MC.

Sizes 1 and 2: Transfer sts to US 1.5 (2.5 mm) needle.

Size 3: Continue with the US 1 (2.25 mm) needle.

Work increase rnd:

> **Size 1 only:** *K6, M1L; repeat from * to 2 sts before the end of the rnd, K2. 9 sts inc'd. 65 sts total.

> **Size 2 only:** [K5, M1L] twice, [K4, M1L] 11 times, K5, M1L, K5. 14 sts inc'd. 78 sts total.

> **Size 3 only:** [K3, M1L] twice, [K4, M1L] 15 times, [K3, M1L] twice. 19 sts inc'd. 91 sts total.

Work rnds 1–35 of the colorwork chart (page 18), joining CC1 and 2 where shown. The chart is worked from right to left, from bottom to the top. The chart is knit 5 (6, 7) times per rnd. See page 171 for tips on how to knit the bobbles.

Cut CC1 and 2.

Knit 1 rnd with MC.

Sizes 1 and 2: Transfer sts back to your US 1 (2.25 mm) needles.

Work decrease rnd with MC:

> **Size 1 only:** *K5, K2tog; repeat from * to 2 sts before the end of the rnd, K2. 9 sts dec'd. 56 sts total.

Size 2 only: [K4, K2tog] twice, [K3, K2tog] 11 times, K4, K2tog, K5. 14 sts dec'd. 64 sts total.

Size 3 only: [K2, K2tog] twice, [K3, K2tog] 15 times, [K2, K2tog] twice. 19 sts dec'd. 72 sts total.

Work the following lace pattern:

Rnd 1:

  Needle 1: K28 (32, 36) sts.

  Needle 2: [K3, yo, K2tog] 5 (6, 7) times, K3 (2, 1).

Rnd 2: Knit all sts.

Rnd 3: Knit all sts.

Repeat rnds 1–3 once more, for a total of 2 times or until you reach your desired length to the heel flap. Continue on to the Heel section of your sock.

Eye of Partridge Heel Flap

The eye of partridge heel is worked flat and knit back and forth using the 28 (32, 36) sts on Needle 1 with CC1. Needle 2 is holding the 28 (32, 36) sts for the instep. You can remove the marker you placed at the beginning.

Row 1 (RS): *Sl1 st purlwise, K1; repeat from * to the end of the row, turn.

Row 2 (WS): Sl1 st purlwise, P to the end of the row, turn.

Row 3 (RS): Sl2 st purlwise, *K1, Sl1; repeat from * to last 2 sts, K2, turn.

Row 4 (WS): Same as Row 2.

Repeat these 4 rows ending on a purl row after a total of 28 (32, 36) rows. There will be 14 (16, 18) edge sts for you to pick up after the heel turn.

Heel Turn

Continuing to use CC1, you will now work short rows to turn your heel.

Row 1 (RS): Sl1, K15 (18, 20), SSK, K1, turn.

Row 2 (WS): Sl1, P5 (7, 7), P2tog, P1, turn.

Row 3 (RS): Sl1, K6 (8, 8), SSK, K1, turn.

Row 4 (WS): Sl1, P7 (9, 9), P2tog, P1, turn.

Continue in this pattern: Sl1, K or P to 1 stitch before the gap created by turning in the previous row, SSK or P2tog to close the gap, K1 or P1, turn. **(For Size 1 only:** On the last 2 rows you will end with the last SSK or P2tog. There will be no sts remaining to K1 or P1). Continue until all stitches have been worked ending with a purl row on the WS. Turn to the right side; you will now have 16 (20, 22) sts left on Needle 1.

Gusset

Cut CC1 and rejoin MC.

Using MC, you will now be picking up stitches along both sides of your heel flap.

Knit across the heel stitches placing a BOR stitch marker after 8 (10, 11) sts (the halfway point).

Pick up and Ktbl 14 (16, 18) sts along the edge of the heel flap. Pick up and knit 1 more stitch at the corner between the heel flap and instep to help prevent a hole in the corner. Place a stitch marker here to help show you when to decrease in the next round or adjust the loop and needles so the heel/gusset sts and instep sts are separated there.

Knit the 28 (32, 36) sts on the instep being held on Needle 2 in the lace pattern to the left. Place a stitch marker after the instep stitches as well, just as you did above.

Pick up 1 stitch in the corner and Ktbl 14 (16, 18) sts along the edge of the heel flap. Knit the first half of the heel to the BOR stitch marker.

You now have a total of 46 (54, 60) heel/gusset sts, 28 (32, 36) instep sts and are working all stitches again in the round. 74 (86, 96) sts on your needles in total.

Gusset Decreases

Rnd 1: Knit to 3 sts before the first stitch marker and K2tog, K1, SM. Knit across the instep stitches, following the next rnd of the lace pattern, to the second marker, SM, K1, SSK. Knit to the BOR stitch marker. 2 sts dec'd.

Rnd 2: Knit all stitches.

Repeat rnds 1 and 2 until you have decreased to 28 (32, 36) heel/gusset sts.

28 (32, 36) instep sts remain on Needle 2. There are now 56 (64, 72) sts in total.

Foot

With MC continue to work every rnd, continuing the lace pattern (page 17), until the foot of your sock measures approximately 1½ inches (4 cm) less than your desired finished length.

Toe

Your stitches are now placed equally on Needles 1 and 2. Needle 1 is holding 28 (32, 36) sts at the bottom of your foot, with 14 (16, 18) sts on either side of the BOR marker. Needle 2 is holding 28 (32, 36) sts at the top of your foot.

With MC, starting from the BOR stitch marker:

Rnd 1 (decrease rnd):

Needle 1: Knit until 3 sts remain, K2tog, K1.

Needle 2: K1, SSK, knit until 3 sts remain, K2tog, K1.

Needle 1: K1, SSK, knit to the BOR stitch marker.

4 sts dec'd.

Rnd 2: Knit all stitches.

Repeat rnds 1 and 2 until there are 20 sts remaining on each needle (40 sts in total).

Continue working only rnd 1 (dec every rnd) until 10 sts remain on each needle (20 sts in total).

Remove BOR stitch marker. Knit 5 stitches to reach the side of the sock. With 10 sts on each needle, join the remaining stitches using Kitchener stitch.

Finishing

Weave in all ends. Soak and block. Repeat instructions for the second sock.

Colorwork Chart

 MC: Eggplant

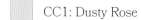 CC1: Dusty Rose

 CC2: Butterscotch

B Make bobble (Eggplant)

Dog Walk

It's no secret that I have a bit of an obsession with cats and seem to pick up random feline friends wherever I go. They have even been known to appear in my living room from time to time. I live on the third floor, so this is quite impressive and surprising! That being said, I am also besotted with my friend's Shiba Inu, whom we refer to as dog cat. It is the cattiest of dogs that I have ever encountered. And as always with things I love, I was determined to create a pair of dog socks in her honor, which would serve as a reminder of our happy walks in the forest together. If you have a doggy pal, I hope you enjoy wearing these with your special friend.

Construction Notes

This sock has a ribbing pattern that starts at the cuff. It then continues after the dog face colorwork pattern on the leg and down to the colorwork dog paw pattern on the foot. Duplicate stitch is used for the eyes and tongue of the dog face. There is a traditional heel flap, turn and gusset.

Sizing

1 (2, 3)

To fit (foot circumference): 8½ (9½, 10½) inches / 20.5–23 (23.5–25, 26–27.5) cm

Finished circumference: 7½ (8½, 9½) inches / 18–20 (20.5–23, 23.5–25) cm

Recommended ease: Approximately 1 inch (2.5 cm) of negative ease.

Leg/foot length can be easily adjusted. See instructions for details.

Sample shown is knit in size 2 for shoe size US 8.5 (EU 39, UK 6), foot circumference 8¾ inches (22.5 cm).

Materials

Yarn

MC and CC2: Fingering weight, GigglingGecko Socklandia Soxs yarn (80% superwash merino wool, 20% nylon), 398 yds (365 m) per 100-g skein

CC1: Fingering weight, Uschitita sock yarn (100% superwash merino wool), 400 yds (366 m) per 100-g skein

Shown in

MC: Army Green (1 skein)

CC1: Aura (1 skein)

CC2: Crème (1 skein)

Any fingering-weight sock yarn can be used for this sock pattern as long as you can obtain the same gauge. A good substitute would be Hue Loco, LolaBean Yarn Co. or an indie dyer of yarn near you.

Needles

For ribbing, heel and toe sections for all sizes: US 1 (2.25 mm), 32-inch (80-cm) circular for magic loop, or DPNs, or two circulars or a 9-inch (23-cm) circular needle (as preferred). Use size required to obtain gauge.

For colorwork:

Size 1: US 1.5 (2.5 mm), 32-inch (80-cm) circular for magic loop, or DPNs, or two circulars or a 9-inch (23-cm) needle (as preferred).

Size 2: US 1 (2.25 mm), 32-inch (80-cm) circular for magic loop, or DPNs, or two circulars or a 9-inch (23-cm) circular needle (as preferred).

(continued)

Gauge

34 sts x 36 rnds = 4 inches (10 cm) for colorwork for sizes 1 and 2.

30 sts x 34 rnds = 4 inches (10 cm) for colorwork for size 3.

32 sts x 42 rnds = 4 inches (10 cm) for stockinette and ribbing for all sizes.

Special Techniques

Knitting Colorwork Socks (page 8)

Duplicate Stitch (page 170)

Kitchener Stitch (page 170)

For all abbreviations, see page 169

Size 3:

Colorwork on leg: US 2 (2.75 mm), 32-inch (80-cm) circular for magic loop, or DPNs, or two circulars or a 9-inch (23-cm) circular needle (as preferred).

Colorwork on foot: US 1.5 (2.5 mm) 32-inch (80-cm) circular for magic loop, or DPNs, or two circulars or a 9-inch (23-cm) circular needle (as preferred).

Important note: *Do check your gauge for fit. Additional sizes can be achieved by going up or down needle sizes.*

Notions

Stitch marker

Scissors

Tapestry needle

Dog Walk Pattern

Cuff

Cast on 56 (64, 72) sts with MC and US 1 (2.25 mm) needle. Divide sts evenly over the two needles and place a marker at the beginning of the rnd. For DPNs, place half of your sts on one needle and divide the other half over two needles. PM for BOR. Join to work in the rnd being careful not to twist sts.

Ribbing Rnd: *K3, P1; rep from * to end of rnd.

Work Ribbing Rnd for a total of 15 rows (approximately 1¼ inches [3 cm]).

Leg

Size 1 only: With MC, using US 1.5 (2.5 mm) needles, work Increase Rnd (page 22).

Size 2 only: With MC, continue with US 1 (2.25 mm) needles and work Increase Rnd (page 22).

Size 3 only: With MC, using US 2 (2.75 mm) needles, work Increase Rnd (page 22).

All sizes

Work increase rnd:

> **Size 1 only:** *K14, M1L; repeat from * to the end of the rnd. 4 sts increased. 60 sts total.

> **Size 2 only:** *K4, M1L; repeat from * to the end of the rnd. 16 sts increased. 80 sts total.

> **Size 3 only:** *K9, M1L; repeat from * to the end of the rnd. 8 sts increased. 80 sts total.

Work rnds 1–26 of Colorwork Chart A (page 24), joining CC1 and CC2 where shown. The chart is worked from right to left, 3 (4, 4) times per rnd. See Special Techniques (page 170) for tips on how to duplicate stitch the eyes and tongue, which you will do once the sock has been completed and you have blocked your sock.

Cut CC1 and CC2.

Knit 1 rnd with MC while transferring sts back to your US 1 (2.25 mm) needles.

Work decrease rnd:

> **Size 1 only:** *K13, K2tog; repeat from * to the end of the rnd. 4 sts decreased. 56 sts total.

> **Size 2 only:** *K3, K2tog; repeat from * to the end of the rnd. 16 sts decreased. 64 sts total.

> **Size 3 only:** *K8, K2tog; repeat from * to the end of the rnd. 8 sts decreased. 72 sts total.

Work in established Ribbing Rnd (K3, P1), for a further 1¾ inches (4.5 cm) or desired length to heel flap.

Heel Flap

The heel flap is worked flat on the 28 (32, 36) sts on Needle 1 with MC. Needle 2 is holding the 28 (32, 36) sts for the instep. You can remove the marker you placed at the beginning.

Row 1 (RS): Sl1 st purlwise, K to the end of the row. Turn.

Row 2 (WS): Sl1 st purlwise, P to the end of the row. Turn.

Repeat these 2 rows ending on a purl row after a total of 28 (32, 36) rows. There will be 14 (16, 18) edge sts for you to pick up after the heel turn.

Heel Turn

Continuing to use MC, you will now use short rows to turn your heel.

Row 1 (RS): Sl1, K15 (18, 20), SSK, K1. Turn.

Row 2 (WS): Sl1, P5 (7, 7), P2tog, P1. Turn.

Row 3 (RS): Sl1, K6 (8, 8), SSK, K1. Turn.

Row 4 (WS): Sl1, P7 (9, 9), P2tog, P1. Turn.

Continue in this pattern: Sl1, K or P to 1 stitch before the gap created by turning in the previous row, SSK or P2tog to close the gap, K1 or P1, turn. **(For size 1 only:** On the last 2 rows you will end with the last SSK or P2tog. There will be no sts remaining to K1 or P1). Continue until all stitches have been worked, ending with a purl row on the WS. Turn to the RS; you will now have 16 (20, 22) sts left on Needle 1.

Gusset

Using MC, you will now be picking up stitches along both sides of your heel flap.

Knit across the heel stitches, placing a BOR stitch marker after 8 (10, 11) sts (the halfway point).

Pick up and Ktbl 14 (16, 18) sts along the edge of the heel flap. Pick up and knit 1 more stitch at the corner between the heel flap and instep to help prevent a hole in the corner. Place a stitch marker here to help show you when to decrease in the next rnd or adjust the loop and needles so the heel/gusset sts and instep sts are separated there.

Work across the 28 (32, 36) sts of the instep (on Needle 2) in the established ribbing pattern. Place a stitch marker after the instep stitches as well, as you did above.

Pick up 1 stitch in the corner and Ktbl 14 (16, 18) sts along the edge of the heel flap. Knit the first half of the heel to the BOR stitch marker.

You now have a total of 46 (54, 60) heel/gusset sts, 28 (32, 36) instep sts and are working all stitches again in the rnd. 74 (86, 96) sts on your needles in total.

Gusset Decreases

Rnd 1: Knit to 3 sts before the first stitch marker and K2tog, K1, SM. Work across the instep stitches in the established ribbing pattern to the second marker, SM, K1, SSK. Knit to the BOR stitch marker. 2 sts dec'd.

Rnd 2: Knit all stitches on Needle 1. Work the established ribbing pattern on Needle 2.

Repeat rnds 1 and 2 until you have decreased to 28 (32, 36) heel/gusset sts. 28 (32, 36) instep sts remain on Needle 2. There are now 56 (64, 72) sts in total.

Foot

With MC continue to work in established pattern (this means the ribbing pattern on the instep and stockinette st on the sole sts), until the foot of your sock measures approximately 3¼ inches (8.5 cm) less than your desired finished length.

For sizes 1 and 3, work the following increase rnd with MC, while transferring the stitches to your US 1.5 (2.5 mm) needles. For size 2, work your increase rnd, continuing to use your US 1 (2.25 mm) needles.

Size 1 only: *K4, M1L; repeat from * to the end of the rnd. 14 sts inc'd. 70 sts total.

Size 2 only: *K10, M1L; repeat from * to 4 sts before the end of the rnd, K4. 6 sts inc'd. 70 sts total.

Size 3 only: *K6, M1L; repeat from * to the end of the rnd. 12 sts inc'd. 84 sts total.

Cut MC.

Work rnds 1–17 of Colorwork Chart B (page 24), joining CC1 and CC2 where shown. The chart is knit 5 (5, 6) times per rnd.

Cut CC1 and CC2.

Work decrease rnd with MC while transferring sts back to US 1 (2.25 mm) needles:

Size 1 only: *K3, K2tog; repeat from * to the end of the rnd. 14 sts dec'd. 56 sts total.

Size 2 only: *K9, K2tog; repeat from * to 4 sts before the end of the rnd, K4. 6 sts dec'd. 64 sts total.

Size 3 only: *K5, K2tog; repeat from * to the end of the rnd. 12 sts dec'd. 72 sts total.

Knit 1 rnd.

Toe

Your stitches are now placed equally on Needles 1 and 2. Needle 1 is holding 28 (32, 36) sts at the bottom of your foot, with 14 (16, 18) sts on either side of the BOR marker. Needle 2 is holding 28 (32, 36) sts at the top of your foot.

Setup rnd: Knit 1 more rnd with MC to the BOR marker.

Rnd 1 (decrease rnd):

Needle 1: Knit until 3 sts remain, K2tog, K1.

Needle 2: K1, SSK, knit until 3 sts remain, K2tog, K1.

Needle 1: K1, SSK, knit to the BOR stitch marker.

4 sts dec'd.

Rnd 2: Knit all stitches.

Repeat rnds 1 and 2 until 20 sts remain on each needle (40 sts in total).

Continue working only rnd 1 (dec every rnd) until 10 sts remain on each needle (20 sts in total).

Remove BOR stitch marker. K5 sts to the side of the sock. With 10 sts on each needle, join remaining stitches using Kitchener stitch.

Finishing

Weave in all ends. Soak and block. And don't forget to add your duplicate stitch eyes and tongue! Repeat instructions for the second sock.

Colorwork Chart A

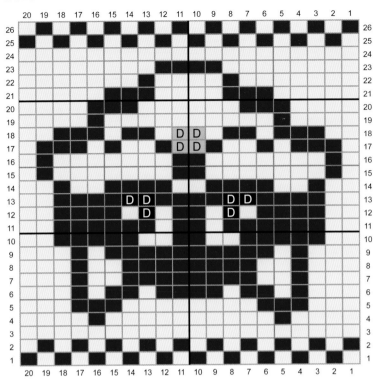

- ■ CC1: Aura
- □ CC2: Crème
- **D** Black Duplicate Stitch
- **D** Pink Duplicate Stitch

Colorwork Chart B

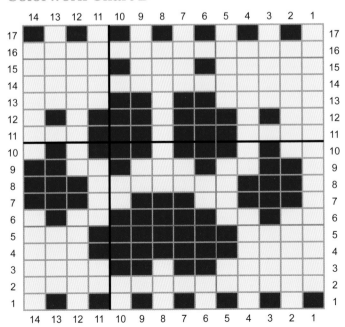

Counting Sheep

What could us knitters love more than warm hand-knitted socks made from wool? Possibly the adorable sheep that provided us with the wool to make them! These little lambs are fun to knit and wear and have textured purl bump sections that represent their adorable woolly coats. Please note that the purl bump sheep stitches are totally optional for the underside of your foot, if you think they might be uncomfortable to step on!

Construction Notes

Knit from the top down starting with a contrasting ribbed cuff, this sock includes an adorable three-colored sheep motif throughout the leg, with little purl stitches for their woolly coats. The heel is constructed as a short row heel.

Sizing

1 (2, 3)

To fit (foot circumference): 8½ (9½, 10½) inches / 20.5 –23 (23.5–25, 26–27.5) cm

Finished circumference: 7½ (8½, 9½) inches / 18–20 (20.5-23, 23.5–25) cm

Recommended ease: Approximately 1 inch (2.5 cm) of negative ease.

Leg/foot length can be easily adjusted. See instructions for details.

Sample shown is knit in size 2 for shoe size US 8.5 (EU 39, UK 6), foot circumference 8¾ inches (22.5 cm).

Materials

Yarn

Fingering weight, West Yorkshire Spinners Signature 4 ply (75% wool, 25% nylon), 437 yds (400 m) per 100-g skein

Shown in

MC: Hydrangea (1 skein)

CC1: Marshmallow (1 skein)

CC2: Butterscotch (1 skein)

Any fingering-weight sock yarn can be used for this sock pattern as long as you can obtain the same gauge. A good substitute would be Sweet-Georgia or Madelinetosh yarns.

Needles

For ribbing, heel and toe: US 1 (2.25 mm), 32-inch (80-cm) circular for magic loop, or DPNs, or two circulars or a 9-inch (23-cm) circular needle (as preferred).

For colorwork: US 1.5 (2.5 mm), 32-inch (80-cm) circular for magic loop, or DPNs, or two circulars or a 9-inch (23-cm) circular needle (as preferred).

Important note: *Do check your gauge for fit. Additional sizes can be achieved by going up or down needle sizes.*

Notions

Stitch marker

Scissors

Tapestry needle

Gauge

34 sts x 38 rnds = 4 inches (10 cm) for colorwork.

36 sts x 44 rnds = 4 inches (10 cm) for ribbing.

Special Techniques

Knitting Colorwork Socks (page 8)

Kitchener Stitch (page 170)

For all abbreviations, see page 169

Counting Sheep Pattern

Cuff

Cast on 56 (64, 72) sts with MC and US 1 (2.25 mm) needle. Divide sts evenly over the two needles and place a marker at the beginning of the round. For DPNs, place half of your sts on one needle and divide the other half over two needles. PM for BOR. Join to work in the rnd being careful not to twist sts.

Ribbing Rnd: *K2, P2; rep from * to end of rnd.

Work Ribbing Rnd for 13 rnds in total or until ribbing measures just about 1¼ inches (3 cm).

Leg

With MC and US 1.5 (2.5 mm) needle (or needle size to achieve gauge in colorwork), work increase rnd:

Size 1: *K14, M1L; rep from * to end of rnd. 4 sts inc'd. 60 sts total.

Size 2: *K8, M1L; rep from * to end of rnd. 8 sts inc'd. 72 sts total.

Size 3: *K6, M1L; rep from * to end of rnd. 12 sts inc'd. 84 sts total.

Work rnds 1–20 of the colorwork chart (page 29), joining CC1 and CC2 where shown. The chart repeats 5 (6, 7) times around the sock. Repeat rnds 1–20 twice, then work rnds 1–10 (you may make as many repeats as you like, to lengthen the leg of your sock; however, you will need to finish after either rnd 10 or 20).

Short Row Heel

Using CC1, size US 1 (2.25 mm) needles and Needle 1 only, you will now work the heel instructions for your size.

Size 1 only (30 sts on Needle 1):

Row 1 (RS): Sl1 [K12, K2tog] twice, turn work to the WS (leaving 1 st unworked). 2 sts dec'd. There are now 28 sts for the heel in total.

Row 2 (WS): Sl1, P25 (leaving 1 st unworked at the end), turn work to the RS.

Row 3: Sl1, K24 (leaving 2 sts unworked at the end), turn work.

Row 4: Sl1, P23 (1 st before the gap), turn work.

Row 5: Sl1, K22 (1 st before the gap), turn work.

Row 6: Sl1, P21 (1 st before the gap), turn work.

Row 7: Sl1, K to 1 st before the gap, turn work.

Row 8: Sl1, P to 1 st before the gap, turn work.

Repeat rows 7 and 8 five more times.

Row 19: Sl1, K to 1 st before the gap, turn work.

Row 20: Sl1, P7, turn work.

You should have 8 purl sts in the center and 10 unworked sts on each side.

The heel now needs to be worked back and forth, closing the gaps that have been created from turning the work.

Row 21 (RS): Sl1, K6, SSK (working together 1 st on either side of the gap), M1L, picking up under the SSK st (do not twist the st), turn work.

Row 22 (WS): Sl1, P7, P2tog, M1Lp, picking up under the P2tog st (do not twist the st), turn work.

Row 23: Sl1, K8, SSK, M1L, turn work.

Row 24: Sl1, P9, P2tog, M1Lp, turn work.

Continue in established pattern for 14 more rows.

Row 39 (RS): Sl1, K24, SSK, M1L, turn work.

Row 40 (WS): Sl1, P25, P2tog, M1Lp, turn work.

Row 41 (RS): Sl1, [K13, M1L] twice, K1. 2 sts inc'd.

There are now 30 sts on Needle 1.

Continue to the Foot section (page 28).

Size 2 only (36 sts on Needle 1):

Row 1 (RS): Sl1, [K6, K2tog] 4 times, K2, turn work to WS (leaving 1 st unworked). 4 sts dec'd. There are now 32 sts for the heel in total.

Row 2 (WS): Sl1, P29 (leaving 1 st unworked at the end), turn work to the RS.

Row 3: Sl1, K28 (leaving 2 sts unworked at the end), turn work.

Row 4: Sl1, P27 (1 st before the gap), turn work.

Row 5: Sl1, K26 (1 st before the gap), turn work.

Row 6: Sl1, P25 (1 st before the gap), turn work.

Row 7: Sl1, K to 1 st before the gap, turn work.

Row 8: Sl1, P to 1 st before the gap, turn work.

Work rows 7 and 8 five more times.

Row 19: Sl1, K to 1 st before the gap, turn work.

Row 20: Sl1, P11, turn work.

You should have 12 purl sts in the center and 10 unworked sts on each side.

The heel now needs to be worked back and forth, closing the gaps that have been created from turning the work.

Row 21 (RS): Sl1, K10, SSK (working together 1 st on either side of the gap), M1L, picking up under the SSK st (do not twist the st), turn work.

Row 22 (WS): Sl1, P11, P2tog, M1Lp, picking up under the P2tog st (do not twist the st), turn work.

Row 23: Sl1, K12, SSK, M1L, turn work.

Row 24: Sl1, P13, P2tog, M1Lp, turn work.

Continue in established pattern for 14 more rows.

Row 39 (RS): Sl1, K28, SSK, M1L, turn work.

Row 40 (WS): Sl1, P29, P2tog, M1Lp, turn work.

Row 41 (RS): [K8, M1L] 4 times. 4 sts inc'd.

There are now 36 sts on Needle 1.

Continue to the Foot section.

Size 3 only (42 sts on Needle 1):

Row 1 (RS): Sl1, [K5, K2tog] 5 times, K3, K2tog, turn work to WS (leaving 1 st unworked). 6 sts dec'd. There are now 36 sts for the heel in total.

Row 2 (WS): Sl1, P33 (leaving 1 st unworked at the end), turn work to the RS.

Row 3: Sl1, K32 (leaving 2 sts unworked at the end), turn work.

Row 4: Sl1, P31 (1 st before the gap), turn work.

Row 5: Sl1, K30 (1 st before the gap), turn work.

Row 6: Sl1, P29 (1 st before the gap), turn work.

Row 7: Sl1, K to 1 st before the gap, turn work.

Row 8: Sl1, P to 1 st before the gap, turn work.

Work rows 7 and 8 six more times.

Row 21: Sl1, K to 1 st before the gap, turn work.

Row 22: Sl1, P13, turn work.

You should have 14 purl sts in the center and 11 unworked sts on each side.

The heel now needs to be worked back and forth, closing the gaps that have been created from turning the work.

Row 23 (RS): Sl1, K12, SSK (working together 1 st on either side of the gap). M1L, picking up under the SSK st (do not twist the st), turn work.

Row 24 (WS): Sl1, P13, P2tog, M1Lp, picking up under the P2tog st (do not twist the st), turn work.

Row 25: Sl1, K14, SSK, M1L, turn work.

Row 26: Sl1, P15, P2tog, M1Lp, turn work.

Continue in established pattern for 16 more rows.

Row 43 (RS): Sl1, K32, SSK, M1L, turn work.

Row 44 (WS): Sl1, P33, P2tog, M1Lp, turn work.

Row 45 (RS): Sl1, [K5, M1L] 6 times, K5. 6 sts inc'd.

There are now 42 sts on Needle 1.

Foot (All Sizes)

Join back in the round with MC and using the US 1.5 (2.5 mm) needles. You will be working with both Needles 1 and 2 again.

Knit 32 (36, 42) sts on Needle 2 back to the beginning of Needle 1 (the BOR). This will be counted as rnd 11 or rnd 1 on the colorwork chart, depending on which sheep you had finished on.

Rejoin CC2 (and eventually CC1) and resume knitting the colorwork chart, starting from either rnd 12 or 2. You may knit the sheep for the bottom of the foot without purl sts if you would prefer to have no texture for this part of the foot.

Continue working the rnds of the colorwork chart until your sock is just over 1½ inches (4 cm) from the end of how long you would like the sock to be. Cut MC and CC2.

Toe

Work decrease rnd with CC1:

Size 1: *K13, K2tog; rep from * to end of rnd. 4 sts dec'd. 56 sts in total.

Size 2: *K7, K2tog; rep from * to end of rnd. 8 sts dec'd. 64 sts in total.

Size 3: *K5, K2tog; rep from * to end of rnd. 12 sts dec'd. 72 sts in total.

Your stitches are now placed equally on Needles 1 and 2. Remove the BOR stitch marker. Needle 1 is holding 28 (32, 36) sts at the bottom of your foot. Needle 2 is holding 28 (32, 36) sts at the top of your foot.

With CC1 and Needle 1, knit 14 (16, 18) sts. Now place the BOR st marker after these sts. This should be in the middle of the sts on Needle 1 at the bottom of your foot. Needle 2 holds the stitches at the top of your foot.

Starting from the BOR stitch marker:

Rnd 1 (decrease round):

   Needle 1: Knit until 3 sts remain, K2tog, K1.

   Needle 2: K1, SSK, knit until 3 sts remain, K2tog, K1.

   Needle 1: K1, SSK, knit to the BOR stitch marker.

   4 sts dec'd.

Rnd 2: Knit all stitches.

Repeat rnds 1 and 2 until 20 sts remain on each needle (40 sts in total).

Continue working only rnd 1 (dec every rnd) until 10 sts remain on each needle (20 sts in total).

Remove BOR stitch marker, then knit 5 stitches to reach the side of the sock. With 10 sts on each needle, join remaining stitches using Kitchener stitch.

Finishing

Weave in all ends. Soak and block. Repeat instructions for the second sock.

Colorwork Chart

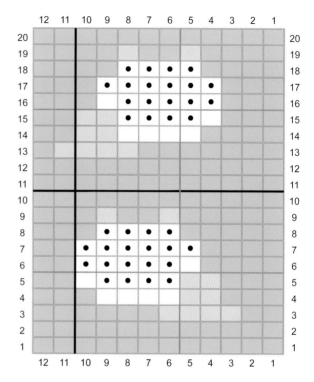

MC: Hydrangea

CC1: Marshmallow

CC2: Butterscotch

• Purl st: Marshmallow

Flutterby Butterfly

These fun Flutterby Butterfly socks embrace the beautiful, bright colors of butterflies (or flutterbys, as my children used to call them!). Not only are butterflies enchanting and fun to watch as they flit happily around the flowers on a warm day, but they also symbolize personal transformation. The butterfly can go through important changes with grace and lightness, something I greatly admire, too. I wanted to capture these magical creatures with a fun pair of socks that also feature colorful "knit faster" stripes. You will finish these socks quickly as you race to complete each stripe!

Construction Notes

Knit from the top down with a ribbed cuff, using three colors, this sock includes a colorwork butterfly pattern section on the leg, followed by three color stripes that start at the leg and continue down through the foot to the toe. These socks are knit with a ribbed heel flap and gusset.

Sizing

1 (2, 3)

To fit (foot circumference): 7 (8½, 9¾) inches / 17–19 (20.5–23, 24–26) cm

Finished foot circumference: 6 (7½, 8¾) inches / 15.5–16.5 (18–20.5, 21.5–23.5) cm

Finished leg circumference: 8 (9, 9¾) inches / 20–21 (22–23, 24–25) cm

Recommended ease: Approximately 1 inch (2.5 cm) of negative ease.

Leg/foot length can be easily adjusted. See instructions for details.

Sample shown is knit in size 2 for shoe size US 8.5 (EU 39, UK 6), foot circumference 8¾ inches (22.5 cm).

Materials

Yarn

Fingering weight, Yarn Love Cinderella Fingering (80% superwash BFL wool, 20% nylon), 185 yds (170 m) per 50-g skein

Shown in

MC: Art Deco (1 skein)

CC1: Antique Teal (1 skein)

CC2: Butterbeer (1 skein)

Any fingering-weight sock yarn can be used for this sock pattern as long as you can obtain the same gauge.

Needles

For ribbing and stockinette: US 1 (2.25 mm), 32-inch (80-cm) circular for magic loop, or DPNs, or two circulars or a 9-inch (23-cm) circular needle (as preferred).

For colorwork: US 1.5 (2.5 mm), 32-inch (80-cm) circular for magic loop, or DPNs, or two circulars or a 9-inch (23-cm) circular needle (as preferred).

Important note: *Do check your gauge for fit. Additional sizes can be achieved by going up or down needle sizes.*

Notions

Stitch marker(s)

Scissors

Tapestry needle

(continued)

Gauge

34 sts x 38 rnds = 4 inches (10 cm) for colorwork.

36 sts x 44 rnds = 4 inches (10 cm) for stockinette and ribbing.

Special Techniques

Jogless Stripes (page 171)

Knitting Colorwork Socks (page 8)

Kitchener Stitch (page 170)

For all abbreviations, see page 169

Flutterby Butterfly Pattern

Cuff

Cast on 56 (64, 72) sts with MC and US 1 (2.25 mm) needle. Divide the sts evenly over the two needles and place a marker at the beginning of the round. For DPNs, place half of your sts on one needle and divide the other half over two needles. PM for BOR. Join to work in the rnd being careful not to twist sts.

Ribbing Rnd: *K1, P1; repeat from * to end of rnd.

Work Ribbing Rnd for a total of 13 rnds or approximately 1¼ inches (3 cm).

Leg

With MC and US 1.5 (2.5 mm) needle (or needle size to achieve gauge in colorwork), work increase rnd:

Size 1: *K6, M1L, K5, M1L; rep from * to 6 sts before the end of the rnd, K6, M1L. 10 sts inc'd. 66 sts total.

Size 2: *K8, M1L; rep from * to the end of rnd. 8 sts inc'd. 72 sts total.

Size 3: *K12, M1L; rep from * to the end of rnd. 6 sts inc'd. 78 sts total.

Work rows 1–33 of the colorwork chart (pages 35–37) relevant for your size, joining CC1 and CC2 where shown. For all sizes, the chart repeats 3 times around the sock. You may wish to add a stitch marker between each repeat.

Using MC and transferring the sts back onto the smaller needle size, work decrease rnd:

Size 1: *K5, K2tog, K4, K2tog; rep from * to 14 sts before the end of the rnd, [K5, K2tog] twice. 10 sts dec'd. 56 sts total.

Size 2: *K7, K2tog; rep from * to the end of the rnd. 8 sts dec'd. 64 sts total.

Size 3: *K11, K2tog; rep from * to the end of the rnd. 6 sts dec'd. 72 sts total.

The sts will now need to be redistributed across the needles, so that a butterfly motif is placed directly in the center front of the sock on Needle 2. These sts will become the instep.

With CC2, knit 14 (16, 18) sts. There are 42 (48, 54) sts remaining until the end of the rnd.

Readjust these sts on the needles so that the first 28 (32, 36) sts are on Needle 2 and the last 14 (16, 18) sts go onto Needle 1. There are now 28 (32, 36) sts on Needle 2 and 28 (32, 36) sts on Needle 1. The BOR is now in the middle of Needle 1. This is the back of the sock which will eventually be used to create the heel, after the leg of the sock has been completed.

Knit the following 42 (48, 54) sts with CC2 until the end of the rnd, with the sts now redistributed across the needles.

Knit 2 more rnds with CC2.

Work the Stripe pattern once.

9-Row Stripe Pattern

Knit 3 rnds CC2.

Knit 3 rnds CC1.

Knit 3 rnds MC.

Cut CC1 and CC2.

Continue to the Ribbed Heel Flap section.

Ribbed Heel Flap

The heel flap is worked flat on the 28 (32, 36) sts on Needle 1 with MC. Needle 2 is holding the 28 (32, 36) sts for the instep. You can remove the marker you placed at the beginning.

Row 1 (RS): *Sl1 st purlwise, K1; repeat from * to the end of the row. Turn.

Row 2 (WS): *Sl1 st purlwise, P1; repeat from * to the end of the row. Turn.

Repeat these 2 rows ending on a purl row after a total of 28 (32, 36) rows. There will be 14 (16, 18) edge sts for you to pick up after you have worked the heel turn.

Heel Turn

Using CC2, you will now use short rows to turn your heel.

Row 1 (RS): Sl1, K15 (18, 20), SSK, K1. Turn.

Row 2 (WS): Sl1, P5 (7, 7), P2tog, P1. Turn.

Row 3 (RS): Sl1, K6 (8, 8), SSK, K1. Turn.

Row 4 (WS): Sl1, P7 (9, 9), P2tog, P1. Turn.

Continue in this pattern: Sl1, K or P to 1 stitch before the gap created by turning in the previous row, SSK or P2tog to close the gap, K1 or P1, turn. (**For size 1 only:** On the last 2 rows you will end with the last SSK or P2tog. There will be no sts remaining to K1 or P1). Continue until all stitches have been worked, ending with a purl row on the WS. Turn to the RS; you will now have 16 (20, 22) sts left on Needle 1.

Gusset

You will now be picking up stitches along both sides of your heel flap.

With CC2, knit 8 (10, 11) sts (the halfway point) and place the new BOR marker.

Rejoin CC1 and knit to the end of the heel sts, then pick up and Ktbl 14 (16, 18) sts along the edge of the heel flap. Pick up and knit 1 more stitch at the corner between the heel flap and instep to help prevent a hole in the corner. Place a stitch marker here to help show you when to decrease in the next round or adjust the loop and needles so the heel/gusset sts and instep sts are separated there.

Knit the 28 (32, 36) sts on the instep being held on Needle 2. Place a stitch marker after the instep stitches as well, just as you did above.

Pick up 1 stitch in the corner and Ktbl 14 (16, 18) sts along the edge of the heel flap. Knit the first half of the heel to the BOR stitch marker.

Foot

Continue to work the 9-Row Stripe pattern until the foot of your sock measures approximately 1½ inches (4 cm) from the desired finished length of your sock, finishing on either a CC1 or CC2 stripe.

Cut CC1 and CC2.

Toe

Your stitches are now placed equally on Needles 1 and 2. Needle 1 is holding 28 (32, 36) sts at the bottom of your foot, with 14 (16, 18) sts on either side of the BOR marker. Needle 2 is holding 28 (32, 36) sts at the top of your foot.

Setup rnd: Knit 1 more rnd with MC to the BOR marker.

Rnd 1 (decrease round):

  Needle 1: Knit until 3 sts remain, K2tog, K1.

  Needle 2: K1, SSK, knit until 3 sts remain, K2tog, K1.

  Needle 1: K1, SSK, knit to the BOR stitch marker.

  4 sts dec'd.

Rnd 2: Knit all stitches.

Repeat rnds 1 and 2 until there are 20 sts remaining on each needle (40 sts in total).

Continue working only rnd 1 (dec every rnd) until 10 sts remain on each needle (20 sts in total).

Remove BOR stitch marker. Knit 5 stitches to reach the side of the sock. With 10 sts on each needle, join remaining stitches using Kitchener stitch.

Finishing

Weave in all ends. Soak and block. Repeat instructions for the second sock.

You now have a total of 46 (54, 60) heel/gusset sts, 28 (32, 36) instep sts and are working all stitches again in the round. 74 (86, 96) sts on your needles in total.

Gusset Decreases

Rnd 1: Using CC1 (to maintain the stripe pattern) knit to 3 sts before the first stitch marker, K2tog, K1, SM. Work across the instep stitches to the second marker, SM, K1, SSK. Knit to the BOR stitch marker.

Rnd 2: Using CC1, knit all stitches.

Repeat rnds 1 and 2 (while continuing to alternate the 9-Row Stripe pattern [page 33] using MC, CC2 and CC1) until you have decreased to 28 (32, 36) heel/gusset sts. 28 (32, 36) instep sts remain on Needle 2. There are now 56 (64, 72) sts in total.

Colorwork Chart – Size 1 Only

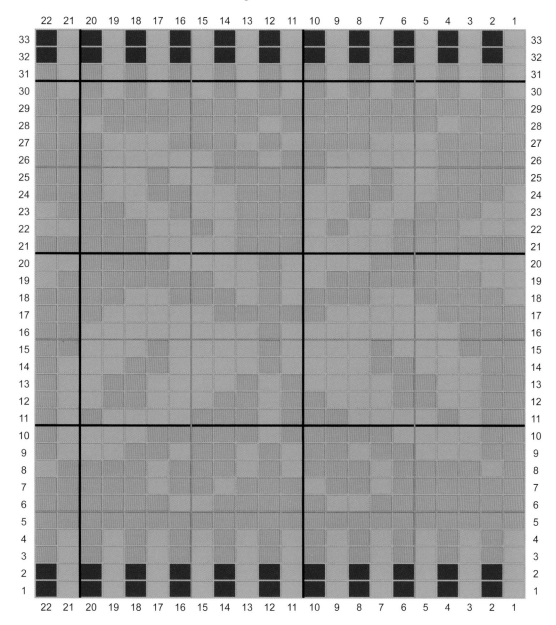

■ MC: Art Deco

□ CC1: Antique Teal

▨ CC2: Butterbeer

Colorwork Chart – Size 2 Only

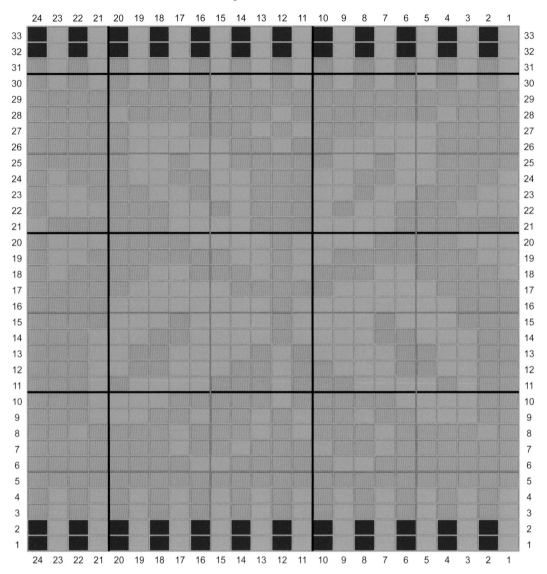

MC: Art Deco

CC1: Antique Teal

CC2: Butterbeer

Colorwork Chart – Size 3 Only

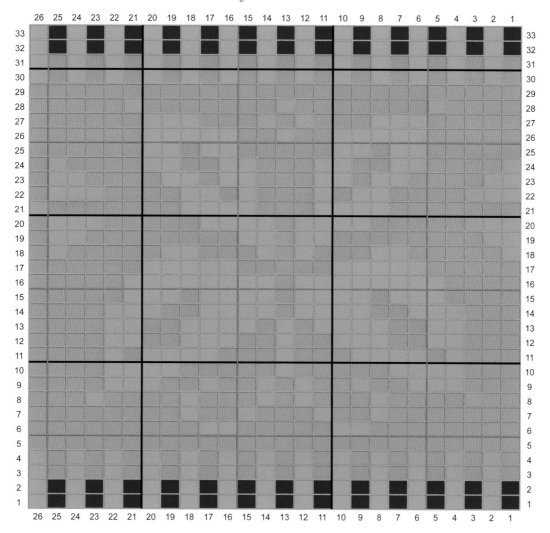

MC: Art Deco

CC1: Antique Teal

CC2: Butterbeer

Swan Lake

When we first moved to Switzerland, I was quite shocked to learn that we can experience very warm summers, as I had imagined eternal snowy mountains and pine forests. And nothing is more refreshing or welcome during a heat wave than a dip in a cool Swiss lake on a hot summer's evening. Inspired by the swans who kindly share the many beautiful lakes with us, I felt these graceful creatures would create an elegant and fun-to-knit pair of socks.

Construction Notes

Knit from the top down with a ribbed cuff, this sock includes a swan colorwork pattern on the leg (with optional duplicate stitch sections for the eyes and beak) and finishes with a little simple colorwork detail before the toe is knitted. These socks are knit with a ribbed heel flap and gusset.

Sizing

1 (2, 3)

To fit (foot circumference): 7½ (8½, 9½) inches / 18–20 (20.5–23, 23.5–25) cm

Finished circumference: 6½ (7½, 8½) inches / 15.5–17.5 (18–20, 20.5–23) cm

Recommended ease: Approximately 1 inch (2.5 cm) of negative ease.

Leg/foot length can be easily adjusted. See instructions for details.

Sample shown is knit in size 2 for shoe size US 8.5 (EU 39, UK 6), foot circumference 8¾ inches (22.5 cm).

Materials

Yarn

Fingering weight, GigglingGecko Socklandia Soxs yarn (80% superwash merino wool, 20% nylon), 398 yds (365 m) per 100-g skein

Shown in

MC: Lake Zürich (1 skein)

CC: Marina Mist (1 skein)

Scrap fingering-weight yarn of black and orange for swan's eye and beak.

Any fingering-weight sock yarn can be used for this sock pattern as long as you can obtain the same gauge. A good substitute would be any hand-dyed sock yarn from an indie dyer near you.

Needles

For ribbing and stockinette: US 1 (2.25 mm), 32-inch (80-cm) circular for magic loop, or DPNs, or two circulars or a 9-inch (23-cm) circular needle (as preferred).

For colorwork: US 1.5 (2.5 mm), 32-inch (80-cm) circular for magic loop, or DPNs, or two circulars or a 9-inch (23-cm) circular needle (as preferred).

Important note: *Do check your gauge for fit. Additional sizes can be achieved by going up or down needle sizes.*

Notions

Stitch marker

Scissors

Tapestry needle

(continued)

Gauge

34 sts x 36 rnds = 4 inches (10 cm) for colorwork for size 1 only.

38 sts x 38 rnds = 4 inches (10 cm) for colorwork on leg for sizes 2 and 3.

34 sts x 28 rnds = 4 inches (10 cm) for colorwork on foot for sizes 2 and 3.

32 sts x 42 rnds = 4 inches (10 cm) for stockinette and ribbing for all sizes.

Special Techniques

Knitting Colorwork Socks (page 8)

Kitchener Stitch (page 170)

Duplicate Stitch (page 170)

For all abbreviations, see page 169

Swan Lake Pattern

Cuff

Cast on 56 (64, 72) sts with MC and US 1 (2.25 mm) needle. Divide sts evenly over the two needles and place a marker at the beginning of the rnd. For DPNs, place half of your sts on one needle and divide the other half over two needles. PM for BOR. Join to work in the rnd being careful not to twist sts.

Ribbing Rnd: *K1, P1; repeat from * to end of rnd.

Work Ribbing Rnd for a total of 13 rows (1¼ inches [3 cm]).

Leg

Knit 1 rnd with MC. For size 1 only, transfer sts to US 1.5 (2.5 mm) needles. For all other sizes, continue with the needles you are using.

Work increase rnd:

Size 1: *K7, M1L; repeat from * to the end of the rnd. 8 sts inc'd. 64 sts total.

Size 2: *K4, M1L; repeat from * to the end of the rnd. 16 sts inc'd. 80 sts total.

Size 3: *K3, M1L; repeat from * to the end of the rnd. 24 sts inc'd. 96 sts total.

Knit 1 rnd with MC.

Begin Colorwork Chart A (page 43), joining CC where shown. The chart is worked from right to left, from bottom to the top. The chart is knit 4 (5, 6) times per rnd. See Special Techniques (page 170) for tips on how to duplicate stitch the eyes and beak, which you will do once the sock has been completed and you have blocked your sock.

Work chart once. Cut CC.

Knit 1 rnd with MC. For size 1, transfer sts back to your US 1 (2.25 mm) needles.

Work decrease rnd with MC and US 1 (2.25 mm) needles:

Size 1: *K6, K2tog; repeat from * to the end of the rnd. 8 sts dec'd. 56 sts total.

Size 2: *K3, K2tog; repeat from * to the end of the rnd. 16 sts dec'd. 64 sts total.

Size 3: *K2, K2tog; repeat from * to the end of the rnd. 24 sts dec'd. 72 sts total.

Knit a further 1¾ inches (4.5 cm) or desired length to heel flap.

Ribbed Heel Flap

The ribbed heel is worked flat with the 28 (32, 36) sts on Needle 1 with MC. Needle 2 is holding the 28 (32, 36) sts for the instep. You can remove the marker you placed at the beginning.

Row 1 (RS): P3, *Sl1 st purlwise, K1; repeat from * to 3 sts before the end of the row, P3, turn.

Row 2 (WS): Sl1 st purlwise, P until the end of the row, turn.

Repeat these 2 rows, ending on a purl row after a total of 28 (32, 36) rows. There will be 14 (16, 18) edge sts for you to pick up after you have worked the heel turn.

Heel Turn

Continuing to use MC, you will now use short rows to turn your heel.

Row 1 (RS): Sl1, K15 (18, 20), SSK, K1, turn.

Row 2 (WS): Sl1, P5 (7, 7), P2tog, P1, turn.

Row 3 (RS): Sl1, K6 (8, 8), SSK, K1, turn.

Row 4 (WS): Sl1, P7 (9, 9), P2tog, P1, turn.

Continue in this pattern: Sl1, K or P to 1 stitch before the gap created by turning in the previous row, SSK or P2tog to close the gap, K1 or P1, turn. (**For size 1 only:** On the last 2 rows you will end with the last SSK or P2tog. There will be no sts remaining to K1 or P1). Continue until all stitches have been worked, ending with a purl row on the WS. Turn to the RS; you will now have 16 (20, 22) sts left on Needle 1.

Gusset

You will be picking up stitches along both sides of your heel flap using MC.

Knit across the heel stitches, placing a BOR stitch marker after 8 (10, 11) stitches (the halfway point).

Pick up and Ktbl 14 (16, 18) sts along the edge of the heel flap. Pick up and knit 1 more stitch at the corner between the heel flap and instep to help prevent a hole in the corner. Place a stitch marker here to help show you when to decrease in the next rnd or adjust the loop and needles so the heel/gusset sts and instep sts are separated there.

Knit the 28 (32, 36) sts on the instep (on Needle 2). Place a stitch marker after the instep stitches as well, as you did above.

Pick up 1 stitch in the corner and Ktbl 14 (16, 18) sts along the edge of the heel flap. Knit the first half of the heel to the BOR stitch marker.

You now have a total of 46 (54, 60) heel/gusset sts, 28 (32, 36) instep sts and are working all stitches again in the round. 74 (86, 96) sts on your needles in total.

Gusset Decreases

Rnd 1: Knit to 3 sts before the first stitch marker and K2tog, K1, knit across the instep stitches to the second marker, K1, SSK. Knit to the BOR stitch marker. 2 sts dec'd.

Rnd 2: Knit all stitches.

Repeat rnds 1 and 2 until you have decreased to 28 (32, 36) heel/gusset sts.

28 (32, 36) instep sts remain on Needle 2. There are now 56 (64, 72) sts in total.

Foot

With MC continue to knit every rnd until the foot of your sock measures approximately 2 inches (5 cm) less than your desired finished length.

Work increase rnd (while transferring sts to US 1.5 [2.5 mm] needles):

Size 1: *K7, M1L; repeat from * to the end of the rnd. 8 sts inc'd. 64 sts total.

Size 2: *K8, M1L; repeat from * to the end of the rnd. 8 sts inc'd. 72 sts total.

Size 3: *K6, M1L; repeat from * to the end of the rnd. 12 sts inc'd. 84 sts total.

Knit 1 rnd.

Work rnds 1–3 of Colorwork Chart B (page 43), joining CC where shown. The chart is worked from right to left, from bottom to the top. The chart is knit 16 (18, 21) times per rnd.

Cut CC.

With MC knit 1 round while transferring sts back to the US 1 (2.25 mm) needles.

Work decrease rnd:

Size 1: *K6, K2tog; repeat from * to the end of the rnd. 8 sts dec'd. 56 sts total.

Size 2: *K7, K2tog; repeat from * to the end of the rnd. 8 sts dec'd. 64 sts total.

Size 3: *K5, K2tog; repeat from * to the end of the rnd. 12 sts dec'd. 72 sts total.

Toe

Your stitches are now placed equally on Needles 1 and 2. Needle 1 is holding 28 (32, 36) sts at the bottom of your foot, with 14 (16, 18) sts on either side of the BOR marker. Needle 2 is holding 28 (32, 36) sts at the top of your foot.

For all sizes:

Starting from the BOR stitch marker:

Rnd 1 (decrease rnd):

Needle 1: Knit until 3 sts remain, K2tog, K1.

Needle 2: K1, SSK, knit until 3 sts remain, K2tog, K1.

Needle 1: K1, SSK, knit to the BOR stitch marker.

4 sts dec'd.

Rnd 2: Knit all stitches.

Repeat rnds 1 and 2 until there are 20 sts remaining on each needle (40 sts in total).

Continue working only rnd 1 (dec every rnd) until 10 sts remain on each needle (20 sts in total).

Remove BOR stitch marker. Knit 5 stitches to reach the side of the sock. With 10 sts on each needle, join the remaining stitches using Kitchener stitch.

Finishing

Weave in all ends. Soak and block. And don't forget to add your duplicate stitch eyes and beak! Repeat instructions for the second sock.

Colorwork Chart A

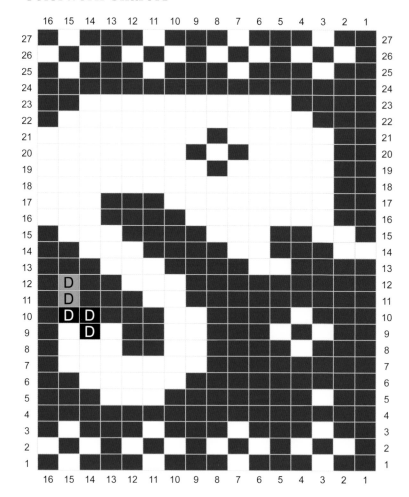

Colorwork Chart B

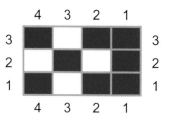

■ MC: Lake Zürich

□ CC: Marina Mist

D Orange Duplicate Stitch

D Black Duplicate Stitch

Flower Power

If you're anything like me, you might be terrible at growing flowers but still crave having them around. Or maybe you are an avid gardener and want flowers on your feet to match your rosebushes or beds of tulips. I think we all love and appreciate flowers all year round wherever we live, whether we are successful gardeners or not. With that in mind, I designed these five sock patterns as a fun, colorful collection dedicated to some of my favorite flowers; I hope they'll become not only some of your favorite flowers, but some of your favorite socks, too!

Blooming Lavender

Lavender is a beautiful herb that originated in North Africa and the Mediterranean mountains but is now grown worldwide. It not only has a pretty flower that can create entire fields of purple in the summer but has a distinctive perfumed scent too. The plant also has many positive medicinal properties and is believed to help with anxiety and insomnia and promote relaxation. I hope these socks help you feel relaxed when you are knitting them up!

Construction Notes

These socks are knit from the cuff down with a twisted ribbed cuff and an eye of partridge heel flap and gusset. They also have a section of colorwork on the leg and a section before the toe.

Sizing

1 (2, 3)

To fit (foot circumference): 7 (8½, 9½) inches / 17–19 (20.5–23, 23.5–25) cm

Finished circumference: 6 (7½, 8½) inches / 14.5–16.5 (18–20, 20.5-23) cm

Recommended ease: Approximately 1 inch (2.5 cm) of negative ease.

Leg/foot length can be easily adjusted. See instructions for details.

Sample shown is knit in size 2 for shoe size US 8.5 (EU 39, UK 6), foot circumference 8¾ inches (22.5 cm).

Materials

Yarn

Fingering weight, Yarn Love Cinderella Fingering (80% superwash BFL wool, 20% nylon), 370 yds (338 m) per 100-g skein.

Shown in

MC: Lupines (1 skein)

CC1: Majesty (1 skein)

CC2: Martini (1 skein)

Any fingering-weight sock yarn can be used for this sock pattern as long as you can obtain the same gauge.

Needles

For ribbing and stockinette: US 1 (2.25 mm), 32-inch (80-cm) circular for magic loop, or DPNs, or two circulars or a 9-inch (23-cm) circular needle (as preferred).

For colorwork: US 1.5 (2.5 mm), 32-inch (80-cm) circular for magic loop, or DPNs, or two circulars or a 9-inch (23-cm) circular needle (as preferred).

Important note: *Do check your gauge for fit. Additional sizes can be achieved by going up or down needle sizes.*

Notions

Stitch marker

Scissors

Tapestry needle

Gauge

34 sts x 38 rnds = 4 inches (10 cm) for colorwork.

36 sts x 44 rnds = 4 inches (10 cm) for ribbing and stockinette.

Special Techniques

Knitting Colorwork Socks (page 8)

Kitchener Stitch (page 170)

For all abbreviations, see page 169

Blooming Lavender Pattern

Cuff

Cast on 56 (64, 72) sts with MC and US 1 (2.25 mm) needle. Divide sts evenly over the two needles and place a marker at the beginning of the round. For DPNs, place half of your sts on one needle and divide the other half over two needles. PM for BOR. Join to work in the rnd being careful not to twist sts.

Ribbing Rnd: *K1, P1; repeat from * to the end of the rnd.

Work Ribbing Rnd for a total of 15 rows (approximately 1½ inches [4 cm]).

Leg

With MC and US 1.5 (2.5 mm) needle (or needle size to achieve gauge in colorwork), work increase rnd:

Size 1: *K14, M1L; rep from * to the end of rnd. 4 sts inc'd. 60 sts total.

Size 2: *K8, M1L; rep from * to the end of rnd. 8 sts inc'd. 72 sts total.

Size 3: *K6, M1L, rep from * to the end of rnd. 12 sts inc'd. 84 sts total.

Work Rnds 1–37 of Colorwork Chart A (page 50), joining CC1 and CC2 where shown. The chart is worked from right to left, from the bottom to the top. The chart is knit 5 (6, 7) times per rnd.

Cut CC1 and CC2.

Knit 1 rnd with MC.

Work decrease rnd with MC and US 1 (2.25 mm) needles:

Size 1: *K13, K2tog; rep from * to end of rnd. 4 sts dec'd. 56 sts in total.

Size 2: *K7, K2tog; rep from * to end of rnd. 8 sts dec'd. 64 sts in total.

Size 3: *K5, K2tog; rep from * to end of rnd. 12 sts dec'd. 72 sts in total.

Knit 1 rnd with MC.

Eye of Partridge Heel Flap

The eye of partridge heel is worked flat and knit back and forth using the 28 (32, 36) sts on Needle 1 with CC1. Needle 2 is holding the 28 (32, 36) sts for the instep. You can remove the marker you placed at the beginning.

Row 1 (RS): *Sl1 st purlwise, K1; repeat from * to the end of the row, turn.

Row 2 (WS): Sl1 st purlwise, P to the end of the row, turn.

Row 3 (RS): Sl2 st purlwise, *K1, Sl1; repeat from * to last 2 sts, K2, turn.

Row 4: (WS) Same as Row 2.

Repeat these 4 rows ending on a purl row after a total of 28 (32, 36) rows. There will be 14 (16, 18) edge sts for you to pick up after the heel turn.

Heel Turn

Continuing to use CC1, you will now use short rows to turn your heel.

Row 1 (RS): Sl1, K15 (18, 20), SSK, K1, turn.

Row 2 (WS): Sl1, P5 (7, 7), P2tog, P1, turn.

Row 3 (RS): Sl1, K6 (8, 8), SSK, K1, turn.

Row 4 (WS): Sl1, P7 (9, 9), P2tog, P1, turn.

Continue in this pattern: Sl1, K or P to 1 stitch before the gap created by turning in the previous row, SSK or P2tog to close the gap, K1 or P1, turn. (**For size 1 only:** On the last 2 rows you will end with the last SSK or P2tog. There will be no sts remaining to K1 or P1.) Continue until all stitches have been worked, ending with a purl row on the WS. Turn to the right side. You will now have 16 (20, 22) sts left on Needle 1.

Gusset

Cut CC1 and rejoin MC.

Using MC, you will now be picking up stitches along both sides of your heel flap.

Knit across the heel stitches, placing a BOR stitch marker after 8 (10, 11) sts (the halfway point).

Pick up and Ktbl 14 (16, 18) sts along the edge of the heel flap. Pick up and knit 1 more stitch at the corner between the heel flap and instep to help prevent a hole in the corner. Place a stitch marker here to help show you when to decrease in the next round or adjust the loop and needles so the heel/gusset sts and instep sts are separated there.

Knit the 28 (32, 36) sts on the instep being held on Needle 2. Place a stitch marker after the instep stitches as well, just as you did above.

Pick up 1 stitch in the corner and Ktbl 14 (16, 18) sts along the edge of the heel flap. Knit the first half of the heel to the BOR stitch marker.

You now have a total of 46 (54, 60) heel/gusset sts, 28 (32, 36) instep sts and are working all stitches again in the round. There are 74 (86, 96) sts on your needles in total.

Gusset Decreases

Rnd 1: Knit to 3 sts before the first stitch marker and K2tog, K1, knit across the instep stitches to the second marker, K1, SSK. Knit to the BOR stitch marker. 2 sts dec'd.

Rnd 2: Knit all stitches.

Repeat rnds 1 and 2 until you have decreased to 28 (32, 36) heel/gusset sts.

28 (32, 36) instep sts remain on Needle 2. There are now 56 (64, 72) sts in total.

Foot

With MC, continue to work every rnd until the foot of your sock measures approximately 2 inches (5 cm) less than your desired finished length.

With MC and US 1.5 (2.5 mm) needle, or needle size to achieve gauge in colorwork, work increase rnd:

Size 1: *K14, M1L; rep from * to the end of the rnd. 4 sts inc'd. 60 sts total.

Size 2: *K10, M1L; rep from * to 4 sts before the end of the rnd. K4. 6 sts inc'd. 70 sts total.

Size 3: *K9, M1L; rep from * to the end of the rnd. 8 sts inc'd. 80 sts total.

Work Rnds 1–7 of Colorwork Chart B (page 50), joining CC2 where shown. The chart repeats 6 (7, 8) times around the sock.

On completion of the chart, cut CC2.

Work decrease rnd with MC:

Size 1: *K13, K2tog; rep from * to the end of the rnd. 4 sts dec'd. 56 sts total.

Size 2: *K9, K2tog; rep from * to 4 sts before the end of the rnd. K4. 6 sts dec'd. 64 sts total.

Size 3: *K8, K2tog; rep from * to the end of the rnd. 8 sts dec'd. 72 sts total.

With MC, knit all rnds until your sock is 1½ inches (4 cm) from the desired finished length. If you are already at this point, continue to the Toe section.

Cut MC.

Toe

Your stitches are now placed equally on Needles 1 and 2. Needle 1 is holding 28 (32, 36) sts at the bottom of your foot, with 14 (16, 18) sts on either side of the BOR marker. Needle 2 is holding 28 (32, 36) sts at the top of your foot.

Setup rnd: Knit 1 rnd with CC1 to the BOR marker.

Starting from the BOR stitch marker:

Rnd 1 (decrease rnd):

Needle 1: Knit until 3 sts remain, K2tog, K1.

Needle 2: K1, SSK, knit until 3 sts remain, K2tog, K1.

Needle 1: K1, SSK, knit to the BOR stitch marker.

4 sts dec'd.

Rnd 2: Knit all stitches.

Repeat rnds 1 and 2 until there are 20 sts remaining on each needle (40 sts in total).

Continue working only rnd 1 (dec every rnd) until 10 sts remain on each needle (20 sts in total).

Remove BOR stitch marker. Knit 5 stitches to reach the side of the sock. With 10 sts on each needle, join remaining stitches using Kitchener stitch.

Finishing

Weave in all ends. Soak and block. Repeat instructions for the second sock.

Colorwork Chart B

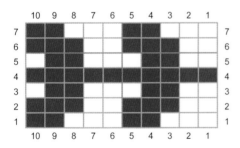

Colorwork Chart A

MC: Lupines

CC1: Majesty

CC2: Martini

Forget-Me-Knot

I have always adored the little forget-me-not flowers with their five tiny, dainty petals. As a young girl, I was often found sitting and admiring them. These perennials are found around the world and symbolize true love, enduring memory and faithfulness. Many legends surround the origins of the forget-me-not and its name. One legend says that when the creator had finished giving out the colors to all the flowers, he heard a tiny whisper, "forget-me-not!" All he had left was a tiny bit of blue, which the little flower was delighted to wear. Inspired by these happy flowers that appear in the spring, these socks are perfect for wearing on a chilly spring morning. And forgive me for the play on words with knot. It is just a reminder to avoid any yarn knots in your socks!

Construction Notes

Knit from the top down with a pretty picot folded edge, this sock includes a simple flower colorwork pattern on the leg, followed by a simple, decorative "lice" pattern which continues until the toe. These socks are knit with a short row heel.

Sizing

1 (2, 3)

To fit (foot circumference): 7 (8½, 9½) inches / 17–19 (20.5–23, 23.5–25) cm

Finished circumference: 6 (7½, 8½) inches / 14.5–16.5 (18–20, 20.5–23) cm

Recommended ease: Approximately 1 inch (2.5 cm) of negative ease.

Leg/foot length can be easily adjusted. See instructions for details.

Sample shown is knit in size 2 for shoe size US 8.5 (EU 39, UK 6), foot circumference 8¾ inches (22.5 cm).

Materials

Yarn

Fingering weight, John Arbon Textiles Exmoor Sock 4ply (60% Exmoor Blueface, 20% Corriedale, 10% Zwartbles, 10% Nylon), 218 yds (200 m) per 50-g skein.

Shown in

MC: Mizzle (2 skeins)

CC1: Whortleberries (1 skein)

CC2: Drumble (1 skein)

Any fingering-weight sock yarn can be used for this sock pattern as long as you can obtain the same gauge. A good substitute would be Yarn Love or SweetGeorgia yarns.

Needles

For picot folded cuff and stockinette: US 1 (2.25 mm), 32-inch (80-cm) circular for magic loop, or DPNs, or two circulars or a 9-inch (23-cm) circular needle (as preferred).

For colorwork: US 1.5 (2.5 mm), 32-inch (80-cm) circular for magic loop, or DPNs, or two circulars or a 9-inch (23-cm) circular needle (as preferred).

Important note: *Do check your gauge for fit. Additional sizes can be achieved by going up or down needle sizes.*

Notions

Stitch marker

Scissors

Tapestry needle

Gauge

34 sts x 38 rnds = 4 inches (10 cm) for colorwork.

36 sts x 44 rnds = 4 inches (10 cm) for stockinette.

(continued)

Special Techniques

Knitting Colorwork Socks (page 8)

Kitchener Stitch (page 170)

Whip Stitch (page 171)

For all abbreviations, see page 169

Forget-Me-Knot Pattern

Picot Folded Cuff

Leaving a 12-inch (30-cm) length of yarn (to sew up the picot edge at the end), cast on 56 (64, 72) sts with MC and US 1 (2.25 mm) needle. Divide sts evenly over the two needles. For DPNs, place half of your sts on one needle and divide the other half over two needles. PM for BOR. Join to work in the rnd being careful not to twist sts.

Rnds 1–10: Knit all sts.

Rnd 11: *K2tog, yo; repeat from * until the end of the rnd.

Rnds 12–22: Knit all sts.

When you are finished knitting the sock or have knitted the leg, you will fold the cuff in half, so the wrong sides are facing one another. The lace detail from rnd 11 creates a pretty picot edge. The cast-on edge needs to be facing rnd 22, just above where the colorwork section begins. Whip stitch the cuff into place using the long length of yarn you left from the cast on.

Leg

With MC and needle size US 1.5 (2.5 mm) or needle size to achieve gauge in colorwork, work increase rnd:

Size 1: *K7, M1L; rep from * to the end of rnd. 8 sts inc'd. 64 sts total.

Size 2: *K8, M1L; rep from * to the end of rnd. 8 sts inc'd. 72 sts total.

Size 3: *K9, M1L; rep from * to the end of rnd. 8 sts inc'd. 80 sts total.

Work rnds 1–26 of the colorwork chart (page 56), joining CC1 and CC2 where shown. The chart repeats 8 (9, 10) times around the sock.

Repeat rnds 19–26 twice more (or as many times as you desire, as long as you end on a rnd 26. Please note, lengthening your sock may require more yarn).

Cut CC1 and CC2.

Short Row Heel

Using MC, size US 1 needles (2.25 mm) and Needle 1 only, you will now work the heel instructions for your size.

Size 1 only (32 sts on Needle 1):

Row 1 (RS): Sl1, [K6, K2tog] 3 times, K4, K2tog, turn work to the WS (leaving 1 st unworked). 4 sts dec'd. There are now 28 sts for the heel in total.

Row 2 (WS): Sl1, P25 (leaving 1 st unworked at the end), turn work to the RS.

Row 3: Sl1, K24 (leaving 2 sts unworked at the end), turn work.

Row 4: Sl1, P23 (1 st before the gap), turn work.

Continue in established pattern for 14 more rows.

Row 39: (RS): Sl1, K24, SSK, M1L, turn work.

Row 40: (WS): Sl1, P25, P2tog, M1Lp, turn work.

Row 41: (RS): Sl1, [K7, M1L] 3 times, K6, M1L.
4 sts inc'd.

There are now 32 sts on Needle 1.

Continue to the Foot section (page 55).

Size 2 only (36 sts on Needle 1):

Row 1 (RS): Sl1, [K6, K2tog] 4 times, K2, turn
work to WS (leaving 1 st unworked). 4 sts dec'd.
There are now 32 sts on your needles for the heel
in total.

Row 2 (WS): Sl1, P29 (leaving 1 st unworked at the
end), turn work to the RS.

Row 3: Sl1, K28 (leaving 2 sts unworked at the end),
turn work.

Row 4: Sl1, P27 (1 st before the gap), turn work.

Row 5: Sl1, K26 (1 st before the gap), turn work.

Row 6: Sl1, P25 (1 st before the gap), turn work.

Row 7: Sl1, K to 1 st before the gap, turn work.

Row 8: Sl1, P to 1 st before the gap, turn work.

Work rows 7 and 8 five more times.

Row 19: Sl1, K to 1 st before the gap, turn work.

Row 20: Sl1, P11, turn work.

You should have 12 purl sts in the center and
10 unworked sts on each side.

The heel now needs to be worked back and forth,
closing the gaps that have been created from turning
the work.

Row 21 (RS): Sl1, K10, SSK (working together 1 st
on either side of the gap), M1L, picking up under the
SSK (do not twist the st), turn work.

Row 22 (WS): Sl1, P11, P2tog, M1Lp, picking up
under the P2tog st (do not twist the st), turn work.

Row 23: Sl1, K12, SSK, M1L, turn work.

Row 24: Sl1, P13, P2tog, M1Lp, turn work.

Row 5: Sl1, K22 (1 st before the gap), turn work.

Row 6: Sl1, P21 (1 st before the gap), turn work.

Row 7: Sl1, K to 1 st before the gap, turn work.

Row 8: Sl1, P to 1 st before the gap, turn work.

Repeat Rows 7 and 8 five more times.

Row 19: Sl1, K to 1 st before the gap, turn work.

Row 20: Sl1, P7, turn work.

You should have 8 purl sts in the center and
10 unworked sts on each side.

The heel now needs to be worked back and forth,
closing the gaps that have been created from turning
the work.

Row 21 (RS): Sl1, K6, SSK (working together 1 st
on either side of the gap), M1L, picking up under the
SSK st (do not twist the st). Turn work.

Row 22 (WS): Sl1, P7, P2tog, M1Lp, picking up
under the P2tog st (do not twist the st). Turn work.

Row 23: Sl1, K8, SSK, M1L, turn work.

Row 24: Sl1, P9, P2tog, M1Lp, turn work.

Continue in established pattern for 14 more rows.

Row 39 (RS): Sl1, K28, SSK, M1L, turn work.

Row 40 (WS): Sl1, P29, P2tog, M1Lp, turn work.

Row 41 (RS): [K8, M1L] 4 times. 4 sts inc'd.

There are now 36 sts on Needle 1.

Continue to the Foot section.

Size 3 only (40 sts on Needle 1):

Row 1 (RS): Sl1, [K8, K2tog] 3 times, K6, K2tog, turn work to the WS (leaving 1 st unworked). 4 sts dec'd. There are now 36 sts on your needles for the heel in total.

Row 2 (WS): Sl1, P33 (leaving 1 st unworked at the end), turn work to the RS.

Row 3: Sl1, K32 (leaving 2 sts unworked at the end), turn work.

Row 4: Sl1, P31 (1 st before the gap), turn work.

Row 5: Sl1, K30 (1 st before the gap), turn work.

Row 6: Sl1, P29 (1 st before the gap), turn work.

Row 7: Sl1, K to 1 st before the gap, turn work.

Row 8: Sl1, P to 1 st before the gap, turn work.

Work rows 7 and 8 six more times.

Row 21: Sl1, K to 1 st before the gap, turn work.

Row 22: Sl1, P13, turn work.

You should have 14 purl sts in the center and 11 unworked sts on each side.

The heel now needs to be worked back and forth, closing the gaps that have been created from turning the work.

Row 23 (RS): Sl1, K12, SSK (working together 1 st on either side of the gap), M1L, picking up under the SSK (do not twist the st), turn work.

Row 24 (WS): Sl1, P13, P2tog, M1Lp, picking up under the P2tog st (do not twist the st), turn work.

Row 25: Sl1, K14, SSK, M1L, turn work.

Row 26: Sl1, P15, P2tog, M1Lp, turn work.

Continue in established pattern for 16 more rows.

Row 43 (RS): Sl1, K32, SSK, M1L, turn work.

Row 44 (WS): Sl1, P33, P2tog, M1Lp, turn work.

Row 45 (RS): Sl1, [K9, M1L] 3 times, K7, M1L. 4 sts inc'd.

There are now 40 sts on Needle 1.

Foot (All Sizes)

Join back in the round with MC and using the US 1 needles (2.5 mm). You will be working with both Needles 1 and 2 again.

Knit 32 (36, 40) sts on Needle 2 back to the BOR (this will be counted as rnd 19 on the color-work chart).

Rejoin CC1 (and eventually CC2) and resume knitting the colorwork chart, starting with rnd 20. Continue to repeat rnds 19–26 until your sock is 2 inches (5 cm) from the desired length.

Work rnds 1–3 of the colorwork chart.

Cut CC1 and CC2.

Toe

Work decrease rnd with MC:

Size 1: *K6, K2tog; rep from * to end of rnd. 8 sts dec'd. 56 sts in total.

Size 2: *K7, K2tog; rep from * to end of rnd. 8 sts dec'd. 64 sts in total.

Size 3: *K8, K2tog; rep from * to end of rnd. 8 sts dec'd. 72 sts in total.

Your stitches are now placed equally on Needles 1 and 2. Remove the BOR stitch marker. Needle 1 is holding 28 (32, 36) sts at the bottom of your foot. Needle 2 is holding 28 (32, 36) sts at the top of your foot.

With MC and Needle 1, knit 14 (16, 18) sts. Now place the BOR stitch marker after these sts. This should be in the middle of the sts on Needle 1 at the bottom of your foot.

Setup rnd: Knit 1 more rnd with MC to the BOR marker.

Rnd 1 (decrease round):

Needle 1: Knit until 3 sts remain, K2tog, K1.

Needle 2: K1, SSK, knit until 3 sts remain, K2tog, K1.

Needle 1: K1, SSK, knit to BOR stitch marker.

4 sts dec'd.

Rnd 2: Knit all sts.

Repeat rnds 1 and 2 until 20 sts remain on each needle (40 sts in total).

Continue knitting only rnd 1 (dec every rnd) until 10 sts remain on each needle (20 sts in total).

Remove BOR stitch marker. K5 sts to the side of the sock. With 10 sts on each needle, join remaining stitches using Kitchener stitch.

Finishing

Weave in all ends. Soak and block. Repeat instructions for the second sock.

Colorwork Chart

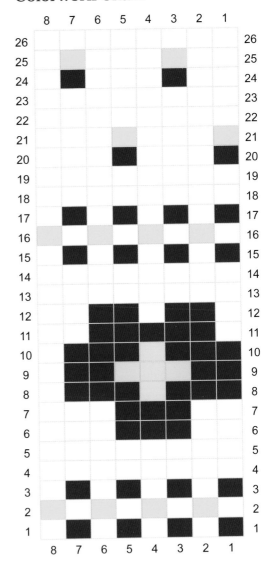

MC: Mizzle

CC1: Whortleberries

CC2: Drumble

Happy Poppy

The summer season is unfortunately not my favorite. I have really tried to embrace everything about it, but I do tend to start longing for the cooler months around about the end of July. I do not cope well with being too hot or being unable to sleep. Living in Europe, we don't have air conditioning, which can make things very unpleasant in a heatwave. I do, however, get very excited when the first poppies start appearing all over the fields here in Switzerland. Poppies are possibly my favorite flower (but this does seem to change with whatever season we're in!). I love how beautiful and bright they are and how they happily grow wildly but are too fragile to pick and bring home. With this in mind, I'll suggest leaving the poppies in the field where they belong for everyone to enjoy and instead, create these happy poppy socks that can be worn throughout every season!

Construction Notes

Knit from the top down with a ribbed cuff, this sock includes an all-over colorwork pattern of a poppy in two colors throughout the leg and foot. The heel is constructed as a short row heel.

Sizing

1 (2, 3)

To fit (foot circumference): 7 (8½, 9½) inches / 17–19 (20.5–23, 23.5–25) cm

Finished circumference: 6 (7½, 8½) inches / 14.5–16.5 (18–20, 20.5–23) cm

Recommended ease: Approximately 1 inch (2.5 cm) of negative ease.

Leg/foot length can be easily adjusted. See instructions for details.

Sample shown is knit in size 2 for shoe size US 8.5 (EU 39, UK 6), foot circumference 8¾ inches (22.5 cm).

Materials

Yarn

Fingering weight, Julie Asselin Nomade (80% superwash merino wool, 20% nylon), 500 yds (457 m) per 115-g skein.

Shown in

MC: Biarritz (1 skein)

CC: Happy (1 skein)

Any fingering-weight sock yarn can be used for this sock pattern as long as you can obtain the same gauge. A good substitute would be Brooklyn Tweed Peerie Yarn.

Needles

For ribbing: US 1 (2.25 mm), 32-inch (80-cm) circular for magic loop, or DPNs, or two circulars or a 9-inch (23-cm) circular needle (as preferred).

For colorwork: US 1.5 (2.5 mm), 32-inch (80-cm) circular for magic loop, or DPNs, or two circulars or a 9-inch (23-cm) circular needle (as preferred).

Important note: *Do check your gauge for fit. Additional sizes can be achieved by going up or down needle sizes.*

Notions

Stitch markers

Scissors

Tapestry needle

Gauge

34 sts x 38 rnds = 4 inches (10 cm) for colorwork.

36 sts x 44 rnds = 4 inches (10 cm) for ribbing.

Special Techniques

Knitting Colorwork Socks (page 8)

Kitchener Stitch (page 170)

For all abbreviations, see page 169

Happy Poppy Pattern

Cuff

Cast on 56 (64, 72) sts with MC and US 1 (2.25 mm) needle. Divide sts evenly over the two needles. For DPNs, place half of your sts on one needle and divide the other half over two needles. PM for BOR. Join to work in the rnd being careful not to twist sts.

Ribbing Rnd: *K1, P1; repeat from * to end.

Work Ribbing Rnd for a total of 13 rnds, approximately 1¼ inches (3 cm).

Leg

With MC and US 1.5 (2.5 mm) needles, or needle size to achieve gauge in colorwork, work increase rnd:

Size 1: *K7, M1L; rep from * to the end of rnd. 8 sts inc'd. 64 sts total.

Size 2: *K8, M1L; rep from * to the end of rnd. 8 sts inc'd. 72 sts total.

Size 3: *K9, M1L; rep from * to the end of rnd. 8 sts inc'd. 80 sts total.

Begin working the colorwork chart for your size (pages 62–63), joining CC where shown. The size 1 chart is on page 62, the size 2 chart is on page 62 and the size 3 chart is on page 63. The chart repeats twice around the sock.

Work rnds 1–32 once, then work rnds 1–16.

Cut CC. Continue on to Short Row Heel instructions.

Short Row Heel

Using MC, size US 1 (2.25 mm) needle and Needle 1 only, you will now work the heel instructions for your size.

Size 1 only (32 sts on Needle 1):

Row 1 (RS): Sl1, [K6, K2tog] 3 times, K4, K2tog, turn work to the WS (leaving 1 st unworked). 4 sts dec'd. There are now 28 sts for the heel in total.

Row 2 (WS): Sl1, P25 (leaving 1 st unworked at the end), turn work to the RS.

Row 3: Sl1, K24 (leaving 2 sts unworked at the end), turn work.

Row 4: Sl1, P23 (1 st before the gap), turn work.

Row 5: Sl1, K22 (1 st before the gap), turn work.

Row 6: Sl1, P21 (1 st before the gap), turn work.

Row 7: Sl1, K to 1 st before the gap, turn work.

Row 8: Sl1, P to 1 st before the gap, turn work.

Repeat Rows 7 and 8 five more times.

Row 19: Sl1, K to 1 st before the gap, turn work.

Row 20: Sl1, P7, turn work.

You should have 8 purl sts in the center and 10 unworked sts on each side.

The heel now needs to be worked back and forth, closing the gaps that have been created from turning the work.

Row 21 (RS): Sl1, K6, SSK (working together 1 st on either side of the gap), M1L, picking up under the SSK st (do not twist the st). Turn work.

Row 22 (WS): Sl1, P7, P2tog, M1Lp, picking up under the P2tog st (do not twist the st), turn work.

Row 23: Sl1, K8, SSK, M1L, turn work.

Row 24: Sl1, P9, P2tog, M1Lp, turn work.

Continue in established pattern for 14 more rows.

Row 39 (RS): Sl1, K24, SSK, M1L, turn work.

Row 40 (WS): Sl1, P25, P2tog, M1Lp, turn work.

Row 41 (RS): Sl1, [K7, M1L] 3 times, K6, M1L. 4 sts inc'd. Turn work.

There are now 32 sts on Needle 1.

Row 42 (WS): Sl1, P31.

Continue to the Foot section (page 61).

Size 2 only (36 sts on Needle 1):

Row 1 (RS): Sl1, [K6, K2tog] 4 times, K2, turn work (leaving 1 st unworked). 4 sts dec'd. There are now 32 sts for the heel in total.

Row 2 (WS): Sl1, P29 (leaving 1 st unworked at the end), turn work to the RS.

Row 3: Sl1, K28 (leaving 2 sts unworked at the end), turn work.

Row 4: Sl1, P27 (1 st before the gap), turn work.

Row 5: Sl1, K26 (1 st before the gap), turn work.

Row 6: Sl1, P25 (1 st before the gap), turn work.

Row 7: Sl1, K to 1 st before the gap, turn work.

Row 8: Sl1, P to 1 st before the gap, turn work.

Work rows 7 and 8 five more times.

Row 19: Sl1, K to 1 st before the gap, turn work.

Row 20: Sl1, P11, turn work.

You should have 12 purl sts in the center and 10 unworked sts on each side.

The heel now needs to be worked back and forth, closing the gaps that have been created from turning the work.

Row 21 (RS): Sl1, K10, SSK (working together 1 st on either side of the gap), M1L, picking up under the SSK st (do not twist the st), turn work.

Row 22 (WS): Sl1, P11, P2tog, M1Lp, picking up under the P2tog st (do not twist the st), turn work.

Row 23: Sl1, K12, SSK, M1L, turn work.

Row 24: Sl1, P13, P2tog, M1Lp, turn work.

Continue in established pattern for 14 more rows.

Row 39 (RS): Sl1, K28, SSK, M1L, turn work.

Row 40 (WS): Sl1, P29, P2tog, M1Lp, turn work.

Row 41 (RS): [K8, M1L] 4 times. 4 sts inc'd. Turn work.

There are now 36 sts on Needle 1.

Row 42 (WS): Sl1, P35.

Continue to the Foot section (page 61).

Size 3 only (40 sts on Needle 1):

Row 1 (RS): Sl1, [K8, K2tog] 3 times, K6, K2tog, turn work to the WS (leaving 1 st unworked). 4 sts dec'd. There are now 36 sts for the heel in total.

Row 2 (WS): Sl1, P33 (leaving 1 st unworked at the end), turn work to the RS.

Row 3: Sl1, K32 (leaving 2 sts unworked at the end), turn work.

Row 4: Sl1, P31 (1 st before the gap), turn work.

Row 5: Sl1, K30 (1 st before the gap), turn work.

Row 6: Sl1, P29 (1 st before the gap), turn work.

Row 7: Sl1, K to 1 st before the gap, turn work.

Row 8: Sl1, P to 1 st before the gap, turn work.

Work rows 7 and 8 six more times.

Row 21: Sl1, K to 1 st before the gap, turn work.

Row 22: Sl1, P13, turn work.

You should have 14 purl sts in the center and 11 unworked sts on each side.

The heel now needs to be worked back and forth, closing the gaps that have been created from turning the work.

Row 23 (RS): Sl1, K12, SSK (working together 1 st on either side of the gap), M1L, picking up under the SSK (do not twist the st), turn work.

Row 24 (WS): Sl1, P13, P2tog, M1Lp, picking up under the P2tog st (do not twist the st), turn work.

Row 25: Sl1, K14, SSK, M1L, turn work.

Row 26: Sl1, P15, P2tog, M1Lp, turn work.

Continue in established pattern for 16 more rows.

Row 43 (RS): Sl1, K32, SSK, M1L, turn work.

Row 44 (WS): Sl1, P33, P2tog, M1Lp, turn work.

Row 45 (RS): Sl1, [K9, M1L] 3 times, K8, M1L. 4 sts inc'd. Turn work.

There are now 40 sts on Needle 1.

Row 46 (WS): Sl1, P39.

Foot (All Sizes)

Join back in the round with MC and CC and US 1.5 (2.5 mm) needle (or needle size to achieve gauge in colorwork). Beginning with Needle 1, resume knitting the chart relevant to your size, on rnd 17. Continue to repeat the chart until the sock is 1½ inches (4 cm) from the desired finished length, even if that means ending the colorwork chart before finishing a full repeat.

If you have finished a full repeat and are not at the above length, you may work the decrease rnd below with MC. After working the decrease rnd, knit a few more rnds of stockinette st with MC until you are at the desired length to work the Toe instructions.

Cut CC.

Toe

Work decrease rnd with MC:

Size 1: *K6, K2tog; rep from * to end of rnd. 8 sts dec'd. 56 sts in total.

Size 2: *K7, K2tog; rep from * to end of rnd. 8 sts dec'd. 64 sts in total.

Size 3: *K8, K2tog; rep from * to end of rnd. 8 sts dec'd. 72 sts in total.

Your stitches are now placed equally on Needles 1 and 2; remove the BOR stitch marker. Needle 1 is holding 28 (32, 36) sts at the bottom of your foot. Needle 2 is holding 28 (32, 36) sts at the top of your foot.

With MC and Needle 1, knit 14 (16, 18) sts. Now place the BOR st marker after these sts. This should be in the middle of the sts on Needle 1 at the bottom of your foot.

Setup rnd: Knit 1 more rnd with MC to the BOR marker.

Rnd 1 (decrease rnd):

Needle 1: Knit until 3 sts remain, K2tog, K1.

Needle 2: K1, SSK, knit until 3 sts remain, K2tog, K1.

Needle 1: K1, SSK, knit to BOR.

4 sts dec'd.

Rnd 2: Knit all sts.

Repeat rnds 1 and 2 until 20 sts remain on each needle (40 sts in total).

Continue working only rnd 1 (dec every rnd) until 10 sts remain on each needle (20 sts in total).

Remove BOR stitch marker. Knit 5 stitches to reach the side of the sock. With 10 sts on each needle, join remaining stitches using Kitchener stitch.

Finishing

Weave in all ends. Soak and block. Repeat instructions for the second sock.

Colorwork Chart – Size 1 Only

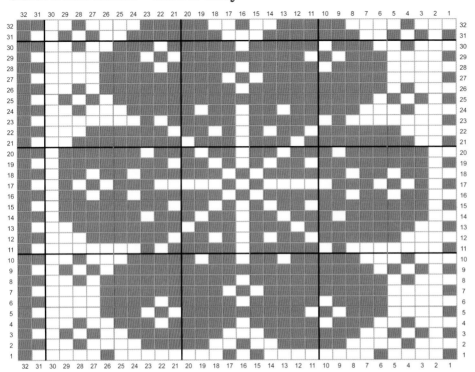

MC: Biarritz

CC: Happy

Colorwork Chart – Size 2 Only

Colorwork Chart – Size 3 Only

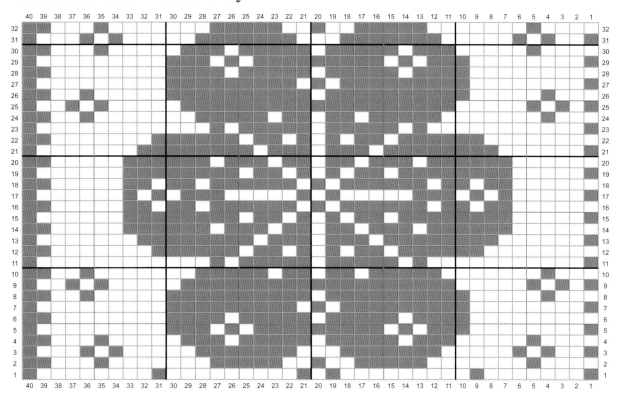

MC: Biarritz

CC: Happy

Raindrops on Roses

The Raindrops on Roses socks feature a classic and easy-to-knit rose flower motif often found in many different knitting patterns from around the world. Knit in two bright colors, the contrast color continues like raindrops throughout the sock. This creates a sock that is very fun and addictive to knit as well as beautiful to wear. And your Raindrops on Roses socks may even end up, as Maria would say in The Sound of Music, *as one of your favorite things . . .*

Construction Notes

These socks are knit from the cuff down with a twisted ribbed cuff and have a short row heel. The stranded colorwork pattern is featured throughout the leg and foot.

Sizing

1 (2, 3)

To fit (foot circumference): 7 (8½, 9½) inches / 17–19 (20.5–23, 23.5–25) cm

Finished circumference: 6 (7½, 8½) inches / 14.5–16.5 (18–20, 20.5-23) cm

Recommended ease: Approximately 1 inch (2.5 cm) of negative ease.

Leg/foot length can be easily adjusted. See instructions for details.

Sample shown is knit in size 2 for shoe size US 8.5 (EU 39, UK 6), foot circumference 8¾ inches (22.5 cm).

Materials

Yarn

MC: Fingering/sock weight, Countess Ablaze Lady Persephone Sock (75% Bluefaced Leicester, 25% nylon), 153 yds (140 m) per 100-g skein

CC: Fingering/sock weight, Qing Fibre Super Soft Sock (80% superwash merino, 10% cashmere, 10% nylon), 96 yds (87.5 m) per 25-g mini skein

Shown in

MC: Take It Offline (1 skein)

CC: Shusui (1 mini skein)

Important Note: *Countess Ablaze has since stopped producing yarn. I would recommend La Bien Aimée, Merino Super Sock in "Peanut Butter & Jelly" as a substitute for MC.*

Any fingering-weight sock yarn can be used for this sock pattern as long as you can obtain the same gauge. Other good substitutes would be LolaBean Yarn Co. or SweetGeorgia yarns.

Needles

For ribbing and heel and toe: US 1 (2.25 mm), 32-inch (80-cm) circular for magic loop, or DPNs, or two circulars or a 9-inch (23-cm) circular needle (as preferred).

For colorwork: US 1.5 (2.5 mm), 32-inch (80-cm) circular for magic loop, or DPNs, or two circulars or a 9-inch (23-cm) circular needle (as preferred).

Important note: *Do check your gauge for fit. Additional sizes can be achieved by going up or down needle sizes.*

Notions

Stitch markers

Scissors

Tapestry needle

Gauge

34 sts x 38 rnds = 4 inches (10 cm) for colorwork.

36 sts x 44 rnds = 4 inches (10 cm) for stockinette and ribbing.

Special Techniques

Knitting Colorwork Socks (page 8)

Kitchener Stitch (page 170)

For all abbreviations, see page 169

Size 2: *K8, M1L; rep from * to end of rnd. 8 sts inc'd. 72 sts total.

Size 3: *K6, M1L; rep from * to end of rnd. 12 sts inc'd. 84 sts total.

Work rnds 1–31 of Colorwork Chart A (page 69), joining CC where shown. The chart repeats 5 (6, 7) times around the sock.

Using MC, work decrease rnd:

Size 1: *K13, K2tog; rep from * to end of rnd. 4 sts dec'd. 56 sts total.

Size 2: *K16, K2tog; rep from * to end of rnd. 4 sts dec'd. 68 sts total.

Size 3: *K19, K2tog; rep from * to end of rnd. 4 sts dec'd. 80 sts total.

Work rnds 1–6 of Colorwork Chart B twice, then work rnds 1 and 2. The chart repeats 14 (17, 20) times around the sock.

Short Row Heel

Using CC, size US 1 (2.25 mm) needle and Needle 1 only, you will now work the heel instructions for your size.

Size 1 only (28 sts on Needle 1):

Row 1 (RS): Sl1, K26, turn work to the WS (leaving 1 st unworked).

Row 2 (WS): Sl1, P25 (leaving 1 st unworked at the end), turn work to the RS.

Row 3: Sl1, K24 (leaving 2 sts unworked at the end), turn work.

Row 4: Sl1, P23 (1 st before the gap), turn work.

Row 5: Sl1, K22 (1 st before the gap), turn work.

Row 6: Sl1, P21 (1 st before the gap), turn work.

Row 7: Sl1, K to 1 st before the gap, turn work.

Row 8: Sl1, P to 1 st before the gap, turn work.

Repeat Rows 7 and 8 five more times.

Row 19: Sl1, K to 1 st before the gap, turn work.

Row 20: Sl1, P7, turn work.

Raindrops on Roses Pattern

Cuff

Cast on 56 (64, 72) sts with MC and US 1 (2.25 mm) needle. Divide sts evenly over the two needles. For DPNs, place half of your sts on one needle and divide the other half over two needles. PM for BOR. Join to work in the rnd being careful not to twist sts.

Ribbing Rnd: *Ktbl, P1; rep from * to the end of the rnd.

Work Ribbing Rnd for a total of 13 rnds or 1¼ inch (3 cm).

Leg

With MC and needle size US 1.5 (2.5 mm), or needle size to achieve gauge in colorwork, work increase rnd:

Size 1: *K14, M1L; rep from * to end of rnd. 4 sts inc'd. 60 sts total.

You should have 8 purl sts in the center and 10 unworked sts on each side.

The heel now needs to be worked back and forth, closing the gaps that have been created from turning the work.

Row 21 (RS): Sl1, K6, SSK (working together 1 st on either side of the gap), M1L, picking up under the SSK st (do not twist the st). Turn work.

Row 22 (WS): Sl1, P7, P2tog, M1Lp, picking up under the P2tog st (do not twist the st), turn work.

Row 23: Sl1, K8, SSK, M1L, turn work.

Row 24: Sl1, P9, P2tog, M1Lp, turn work.

Continue in established pattern for 14 more rows.

Row 39 (RS): Sl1, K24, SSK, M1L, turn work.

Row 40 (WS): Sl1, P25, P2tog, M1Lp, turn work.

Row 41 (RS): Sl1, K27.

There are now 28 sts on Needle 1.

Continue to the Foot section (page 68).

Size 2 only (34 sts on Needle 1):

Row 1 (RS): Sl1, [K14, K2tog] twice, turn work to WS (leaving 1 st unworked). 2 sts dec'd. There are now 32 sts on your needles for the heel in total.

Row 2 (WS): Sl1, P29 (leaving 1 st unworked at the end), turn work to the RS.

Row 3: Sl1, K28 (leaving 2 sts unworked at the end), turn work.

Row 4: Sl1, P27 (1 st before the gap), turn work.

Row 5: Sl1, K26 (1 st before the gap), turn work.

Row 6: Sl1, P25 (1 st before the gap), turn work.

Row 7: Sl1, K to 1 st before the gap, turn work.

Row 8: Sl1, P to 1 st before the gap, turn work.

Work rows 7 and 8 five more times.

Row 19: Sl1, K to 1 st before the gap, turn work.

Row 20: Sl1, P11, turn work.

You should have 12 purl sts in the center and 10 unworked sts on each side.

The heel now needs to be worked back and forth, closing the gaps that have been created from turning the work.

Row 21 (RS): Sl1, K10, SSK (working together 1 st on either side of the gap), M1L, picking up under the SSK (do not twist the st), turn work.

Row 22 (WS): Sl1, P11, P2tog, M1Lp picking up under the P2tog st (do not twist the st), turn work.

Row 23: Sl1, K12, SSK, M1L, turn work.

Row 24: Sl1, P13, P2tog, M1Lp, turn work.

Continue in established pattern for 14 more rows.

Row 39 (RS): Sl1, K28, SSK, M1L, turn work.

Row 40 (WS): Sl1, P29, P2tog, M1Lp, turn work.

Row 41 (RS): [K16, M1L] twice. 2 sts inc'd.

There are now 34 sts on Needle 1.

Continue to the Foot section (page 68).

Size 3 only (40 sts on Needle 1):

Row 1 (RS): Sl1, [K7, K2tog] 4 times, K2, turn work to the WS (leaving 1 st unworked). 4 sts dec'd. There are now 36 sts for the heel in total.

Row 2 (WS): Sl1, P33 (leaving 1 st unworked at the end), turn work to the RS.

Row 3: Sl1, K32 (leaving 2 sts unworked at the end), turn work.

Row 4: Sl1, P31 (1 st before the gap), turn work.

Row 5: Sl1, K30 (1 st before the gap), turn work.

Row 6: Sl1, P29 (1 st before the gap), turn work.

Row 7: Sl1, K to 1 st before the gap, turn work.

Row 8: Sl1, P to 1 st before the gap, turn work.

Work rows 7 and 8 six more times.

Row 21: Sl1, K to 1 st before the gap, turn work.

Row 22: Sl1, P13, turn work.

You should have 14 purl sts in the center and 11 unworked sts on each side.

The heel now needs to be worked back and forth, closing the gaps that have been created from turning the work.

Row 23 (RS): Sl1, K12, SSK (working together 1 st on either side of the gap), M1L, picking up under the SSK (do not twist the st), turn work.

Row 24 (WS): Sl1, P13, P2tog, M1Lp, picking up under the P2tog st (do not twist the st), turn work.

Row 25: Sl1, K14, SSK, M1L, turn work.

Row 26: Sl1, P15, P2tog, M1Lp, turn work.

Continue in established pattern for 16 more rows.

Row 43 (RS): Sl1, K32, SSK, M1L, turn work.

Row 44 (WS): Sl1, P33, P2tog, M1Lp, turn work.

Row 45 (RS): Sl1, [K8, M1L] 4 times, K to end. 4 sts inc'd.

There are now 40 sts on Needle 1.

Foot

Join back in the round with MC and using the US 1.5 (2.5 mm) needles. You will be working with both Needles 1 and 2 again.

Knit 28 (34, 40) sts on Needle 2 back to the BOR (this will count as rnd 3 on Colorwork Chart B).

Continue working Colorwork Chart B, starting with rnd 4 and ending on rnd 8. Now repeat rnds 1–8 until the sock is approximately 2¾ inches (7 cm) from the desired finished length. You can finish on any rnd.

Work rnds 1–7 of Colorwork Chart C (page 69). The chart repeats 14 (17, 20) times around the sock. Cut MC.

Toe

With CC, work this rnd while transferring your sts onto the smaller needle size.

Size 1: Knit 1 rnd.

Size 2: *K15, K2tog; rep from * to end of rnd. 4 sts dec'd. 64 sts in total.

Size 3: *K8, K2tog; rep from * to end of rnd. 8 sts dec'd. 72 sts in total.

Your stitches should now be placed equally on Needles 1 and 2. Remove the BOR stitch marker. Needle 1 is holding 28 (32, 36) sts at the bottom of your foot. Needle 2 is holding 28 (32, 36) sts at the top of your foot.

With CC and Needle 1, knit 14 (16, 18) sts. Place the BOR st marker after these sts. This should be in the middle of the sts on Needle 1 at the bottom of your foot. Needle 2 holds the sts at the top of your foot.

Setup rnd: Knit with CC to BOR marker.

Rnd 1 (decrease rnd):

Needle 1: Knit until 3 sts remain, K2tog, K1.

Needle 2: K1, SSK, knit until 3 sts remain, K2tog, K1.

Needle 1: K1, SSK, knit to BOR.

4 sts dec'd.

Rnd 2: Knit all sts.

Repeat rnds 1 and 2 until 20 sts remain on each needle (40 sts in total).

Continue knitting only rnd 1 (dec every rnd) until 10 sts remain on each needle (20 sts in total).

Remove BOR stitch marker. Knit 5 stitches to reach the side of the sock. With 10 sts on each needle, join remaining stitches using Kitchener stitch.

Finishing

Weave in all ends. Soak and block. Repeat instructions for the second sock.

Colorwork Chart A

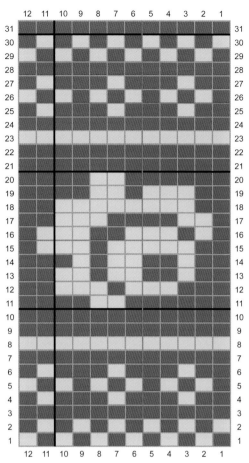

Colorwork Chart B   Colorwork Chart C

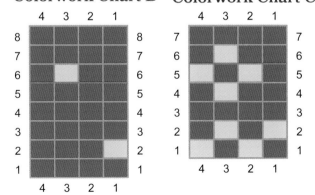

MC: Take It Offline

CC: Shusui

Tiptoe Through the Tulips

I love tulip displays with their many amazing colors. They are one of the first signs that spring is in the air and that flowers, color and life will soon appear again in the garden. I find they are such a welcome treat as winter starts thawing and their green shoots start appearing through the snow. I wanted to celebrate this flower by creating a pair of socks using multi-colored variegated "tulip" color yarn to honor them and that feeling of hope that winter is finally ending and the light of spring is returning.

Construction Notes

Using three colors, these socks are knit from the top down with a ribbed cuff and include a simple decorative colorwork pattern by the cuff and the toe. The tulip motif flows throughout the leg and foot. These socks are knit with a short row heel.

Sizing

1 (2, 3)

To fit (foot circumference): 7 (8½, 9½) inches / 17–19 (20.5–23, 23.5–25) cm

Finished circumference: 6 (7½, 8½) inches / 14.5–16.5 (18–20, 20.5-23) cm

Recommended ease: Approximately 1 inch (2.5 cm) of negative ease.

Leg/foot length can be easily adjusted. See instructions for details.

Sample shown is knit in size 2 for shoe size US 8.5 (EU 39, UK 6), foot circumference 8¾ inches (22.5 cm).

Materials

Yarn

MC and CC2: Fingering weight, Yarn Love Cinderella Fingering (80% superwash BFL wool, 20% nylon), 370 yds (338 m) per 100-g skein

CC1: Fingering weight, Yarn Love Galadriel Sock (80% superwash Corriedale, 20% nylon), 370 yds (338 m) per 100-g skein

Shown in

MC: Conifer (1 skein)

CC1: Cosmos (1 skein)

CC2: Martini (1 20-g mini skein)

Needles

For ribbing, heel and toe: US 1 (2.25 mm), 32-inch (80-cm) circular for magic loop, or DPNs, or two circulars or a 9-inch (23-cm) circular needle (as preferred).

For colorwork: US 1.5 (2.5 mm), 32-inch (80-cm) circular for magic loop, or DPNs, or two circulars or a 9-inch (23-cm) circular needle (as preferred).

Important note: *Do check your gauge for fit. Additional sizes can be achieved by going up or down needle sizes.*

Notions

Stitch markers

Scissors

Tapestry needle

Gauge

34 sts x 38 rnds = 4 inches (10 cm) for colorwork.

36 sts x 44 rnds = 4 inches (10 cm) for stockinette and ribbing.

Special Techniques

Knitting Colorwork Socks (page 8)

Kitchener Stitch (page 170)

For all abbreviations, see page 169

Tiptoe Through the Tulips Pattern

Cuff

Cast on 56 (64, 72) sts with MC and US 1 (2.25 mm) needle. Divide sts evenly over the two needles. For DPNs, place half of your sts on one needle and divide the other half over two needles. PM for BOR. Join to work in the rnd, being careful not to twist sts.

Ribbing Rnd: *K1tbl, P1; repeat from * to the end of the rnd.

Work Ribbing Rnd for a total of 13 rnds, approximately 1¼ inches (3 cm).

Leg

With MC and US 1.5 (2.5 mm) needle (or needle size to achieve gauge in colorwork), work increase rnd:

Size 1: *K14, M1L; rep from * to the end of rnd. 4 sts inc'd. 60 sts total.

Size 2: *K8, M1L; rep from * to the end of rnd. 8 sts inc'd. 72 sts total.

Size 3: *K6, M1L, rep from * to the end of rnd. 12 sts inc'd. 84 sts total.

Work rnds 1–3 of Colorwork Chart B (page 75), joining CC1 where shown. The chart repeats 5 (6, 7) times around the sock. The chart is worked from right to left, from bottom to the top. Now work rnds 1–24 of Colorwork Chart A (page 75), joining CC2 where shown. The chart repeats 5 (6, 7) times around the sock. Knit rnds 1–13 once more and then continue on to the Short Row Heel instructions.

Short Row Heel

Using MC, size US 1 (2.25 mm) needle and Needle 1 only, you will now work the heel instructions for your size.

Size 1 only (30 sts on Needle 1):

Row 1 (RS): Sl1, [K12, K2tog] twice, turn work to the WS (leaving 1 st unworked). 2 sts dec'd. There are now 28 sts for the heel in total.

Row 2 (WS): Sl1, P25 (leaving 1 st unworked at the end), turn work to the RS.

Row 3: Sl1, K24 (leaving 2 sts unworked at the end), turn work.

Row 4: Sl1, P23 (1 st before the gap), turn work.

Row 5: Sl1, K22 (1 st before the gap), turn work.

Row 6: Sl1, P21 (1 st before the gap), turn work.

Row 7: Sl1, K to 1 st before the gap, turn work.

Row 8: Sl1, P to 1 st before the gap, turn work.

Repeat Rows 7 and 8 five more times.

Row 19: Sl1, K to 1 st before the gap, turn work.

Row 20: Sl1, P7, turn work.

You should have 8 purl sts in the center and 10 unworked sts on each side.

The heel now needs to be worked back and forth, closing the gaps that have been created from turning the work.

Row 21 (RS): Sl1, K6, SSK (working together 1 st on either side of the gap), M1L, picking up under the SSK (do not twist the st). Turn work.

Row 22 (WS): Sl1, P7, P2tog, M1Lp, picking up under the P2tog st (do not twist the st), turn work.

Row 23: Sl1, K8, SSK, M1L, turn work.

Row 24: Sl1, P9, P2tog, M1Lp, turn work.

Continue in established pattern for 14 more rows.

Row 39 (RS): Sl1, K24, SSK, M1L, turn work.

Row 40 (WS): Sl1, P25, P2tog, M1Lp, turn work.

Row 41 (RS): Sl1, [K13, M1L] twice, K1. 2 sts inc'd. Turn work.

There are now 30 sts on Needle 1.

Row 42 (WS): Sl1, P29.

Continue to the Foot section (page 74).

Size 2 only (36 sts on Needle 1):

Row 1 (RS): Sl1, [K6, K2tog] 4 times, K2, turn work to the WS (leaving 1 st unworked). 4 sts dec'd. There are now 32 sts for the heel in total.

Row 2 (WS): Sl1, P29 (leaving 1 st unworked at the end), turn work to the RS.

Row 3: Sl1, K28 (leaving 2 sts unworked at the end), turn work.

Row 4: Sl1, P27 (1 st before the gap), turn work.

Row 5: Sl1, K26 (1 st before the gap), turn work.

Row 6: Sl1, P25 (1 st before the gap), turn work.

Row 7: Sl1, K to 1 st before the gap, turn work.

Row 8: Sl1, P to 1 st before the gap, turn work.

Work rows 7 and 8 five more times.

Row 19: Sl1, K to 1 st before the gap, turn work.

Row 20: Sl1, P11, turn work.

You should have 12 purl sts in the center and 10 unworked sts on each side.

The heel now needs to be worked back and forth, closing the gaps that have been created from turning the work.

Row 21 (RS): Sl1, K10, SSK (working together 1 st on either side of the gap), M1L, picking up under the SSK (do not twist the st), turn work.

Row 22 (WS): Sl1, P11, P2tog, M1Lp, picking up under the P2tog st (do not twist the st), turn work.

Row 23: Sl1, K12, SSK, M1L, turn work.

Row 24: Sl1, P13, P2tog, M1Lp, turn work.

Continue in established pattern for 14 more rows.

Row 39 (RS): Sl1, K28, SSK, M1L, turn work.

Row 40 (WS): Sl1, P29, P2tog, M1Lp, turn work.

Row 41 (RS): [K8, M1L] 4 times. 4 sts inc'd. Turn work.

There are now 36 sts on Needle 1.

Row 42 (WS): Sl1, P35.

Continue to the Foot section (page 74).

Size 3 only (42 sts on Needle 1):

Row 1 (RS): Sl1, [K5, K2tog] 5 times, K3, K2tog, turn work to the WS (leaving 1 st unworked). 6 sts dec'd. There are now 36 sts for the heel in total.

Row 2 (WS): Sl1, P33 (leaving 1 st unworked at the end), turn work to the RS.

Row 3: Sl1, K32 (leaving 2 sts unworked at the end), turn work.

Row 4: Sl1, P31 (1 st before the gap), turn work.

Row 5: Sl1, K30 (1 st before the gap), turn work.

Row 6: Sl1, P29 (1 st before the gap), turn work.

Row 7: Sl1, K to 1 st before the gap, turn work.

Row 8: Sl1, P to 1 st before the gap, turn work.

Work rows 7 and 8 six more times.

Row 21: Sl1, K to 1 st before the gap, turn work.

Row 22: Sl1, P13, turn work.

You should have 14 purl sts in the center and 11 unworked sts on each side.

The heel now needs to be worked back and forth, closing the gaps that have been created from turning the work.

Row 23 (RS): Sl1, K12, SSK (working together 1 st on either side of the gap). M1L, picking up under the SSK (do not twist the st), turn work.

Row 24 (WS): Sl1, P13, P2tog, M1Lp, picking up under the P2tog st (do not twist the st), turn work.

Row 25: Sl1, K14, SSK, M1L, turn work.

Row 26: Sl1, P15, P2tog, M1Lp, turn work.

Continue in established pattern for 16 more rows.

Row 43 (RS): Sl1, K32, SSK, M1L, turn work.

Row 44 (WS): Sl1, P33, P2tog, M1Lp, turn work.

Row 45 (RS): Sl1, [K5, M1L] 6 times, K5. 6 sts inc'd.

There are now 42 sts on Needle 1.

Row 46 (WS): Sl1, P41.

Foot (All Sizes)

Join back in the round with MC, CC1, CC2 and US 1.5 (2.5 mm) needle (or needle size to achieve gauge in colorwork). Beginning with Needle 1, resume knitting Colorwork Chart A (page 75), starting with rnd 14 and ending on rnd 24. Continue to repeat Colorwork Chart A until the sock is approximately 1¾ inches (4.5 cm) from the desired finished length, stopping after rnd 13. If necessary, knit a few more rnds with MC to get to this length.

Cut CC2.

Work rnds 1–3 of Colorwork Chart C (page 75). The chart repeats 5 (6, 7) times around the sock.

Cut CC1.

Toe

With MC and using the US 1 (2.25 mm) needle, work decrease rnd:

Size 1: *K13, K2tog; rep from * to end of rnd. 4 sts dec'd. 56 sts in total.

Size 2: *K7, K2tog; rep from * to end of rnd. 8 sts dec'd. 64 sts in total.

Size 3: *K5, K2tog; rep from * to end of rnd. 12 sts dec'd. 72 sts in total.

Your stitches should now be placed equally on Needles 1 and 2. Remove the BOR stitch marker. Needle 1 is holding 28 (32, 36) sts at the bottom of your foot. Needle 2 is holding 28 (32, 36) sts at the top of your foot.

With MC and Needle 1, knit 14 (16, 18) sts. Place the BOR st marker after these sts. This should be in the middle of the sts on Needle 1.

Setup rnd: Knit 1 more rnd with MC to the BOR marker.

Rnd 1 (decrease rnd):

   Needle 1: Knit until 3 sts remain, K2tog, K1.

   Needle 2: K1, SSK, knit until 3 sts remain, K2tog, K1.

   Needle 1: K1, SSK, knit to BOR.

   4 sts dec'd.

Rnd 2: Knit all sts.

Repeat rnds 1 and 2 until there are 20 sts remaining on each needle (40 sts in total).

Continue working only rnd 1 (dec every rnd) until 10 sts remain on each needle (20 sts in total).

Remove BOR stitch marker. Knit 5 stitches to reach the side of the sock. With 10 sts on each needle, join remaining stitches using Kitchener stitch.

Finishing

Weave in all ends. Soak and block. Repeat instructions for the second sock.

Colorwork Chart A

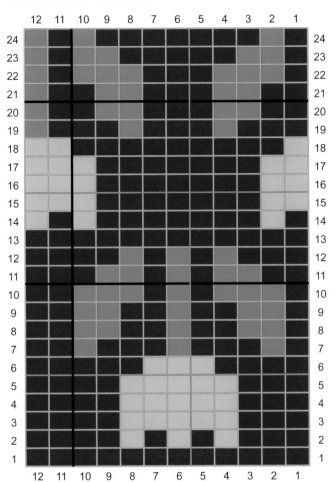

MC: Conifer

CC1: Cosmos

CC2: Martini

Colorwork Chart B

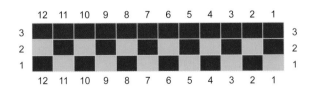

Colorwork Chart C

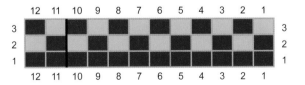

Food, Glorious Food

My knitting designs are often inspired by things I see in everyday life, and food is a big, happy part of my day. I am easily excited by the sight of a bright red chili pepper, a juicy mandarin orange or a hot, steaming cup of coffee first thing in the morning. Whether you are having breakfast, lunch or dinner—or any kind of snack in between!—I am sure wearing fancy food-related socks will bring a smile to your face.

Cherry on Top

"A cherry on top" is the final touch that makes something as beautiful as possible. I feel that's true for these delightful striped socks with fun colorwork cherry motifs. How can we resist cherries, whether they are sweet and fresh off the tree in the summer months, the sour variety in a delicious pie or the warm, wooly version knit on these socks?

Construction Notes

Knit from the top down with a ribbed cuff, this sock includes an original cherry colorwork pattern on the leg, with a smaller berry pattern knit before the toe. These socks are addictive to knit with stripes running throughout the leg and foot. An eye of partridge heel flap and gusset are included.

Sizing

1 (2, 3)

To fit (foot circumference): 7 (8½, 9½) inches / 17–19 (20.5–23, 23.5–25) cm

Finished circumference: 6 (7½, 8½) inches / 14.5–16.5 (18–20, 20.5-23) cm

Recommended ease: Approximately 1 inch (2.5 cm) of negative ease.

Leg/foot length can be easily adjusted. See instructions for details.

Sample shown is knit in size 2 for shoe size US 8.5 (EU 39, UK 6), foot circumference 8¾ inches (22.5 cm).

Materials

Yarn

Fingering weight, Schachenmayr Regia Premium 4-ply Merino Yak (58% Wool, 28% Polyamide, 14% Yak), 437 yds (400 m) per 100-g skein.

Shown in

MC: Mint Meliert (1 skein)

CC1: Himbeer Meliert (1 skein)

CC2: Teal Meliert (1 skein)

Any fingering-weight sock yarn can be used for this sock pattern as long as you can obtain the same gauge. A good substitute would be Sweet-Georgia yarns or Madelinetosh.

Needles

For ribbing and stockinette for all sizes: US 1 (2.25 mm), 32-inch (80-cm) circular for magic loop, or DPNs, or two circulars or a 9-inch (23-cm) circular needle (as preferred).

For size 1 colorwork only: US 1.5 (2.5 mm), 32-inch (80-cm) circular for magic loop, or DPNs, or two circulars or a 9-inch (23-cm) circular needle (as preferred).

For size 2 colorwork only: US 1 (2.25 mm), 32-inch (80-cm) circular for magic loop, or DPNs, or two circulars or a 9-inch (23-cm) circular needle (as preferred).

For size 3 colorwork only: US 2 (2.75 mm), 32-inch (80-cm) circular for magic loop, or DPNs, or two circulars or a 9-inch (23-cm) circular needle (as preferred).

Important note: *Do check your gauge for fit. Additional sizes can be achieved by going up or down needle sizes.*

(continued)

Notions

Stitch marker

Scissors

Tapestry needle

Gauge

34 sts x 38 rnds = 4 inches (10 cm) for size 1 leg colorwork only.

36 sts x 40 rnds = 4 inches (10 cm) for stockinette, ribbing and size 2 leg colorwork.

32 sts x 44 rnds = 4 inches (10 cm) for size 3 leg colorwork only.

Special Techniques

Knitting Colorwork Socks (page 8)

Jogless Stripes (page 171)

Kitchener Stitch (page 170)

For all abbreviations, see page 169

Cherry on Top Pattern

Cuff

Cast on 56 (64, 72) sts with MC and size US 1 (2.25 mm) needles. Divide sts evenly over the two needles and place a marker at the beginning of the round. For DPNs, place half of your sts on one needle and divide the other half over two needles. Join to work in the rnd, being careful not to twist sts.

Ribbing Rnd: *K1, P1; rep from * to end of rnd.

Work Ribbing Rnd for a total of 12 rows, approximately 1¼ inches (3 cm).

Leg

Knit 1 rnd with MC. For sizes 1 and 3 only, transfer the sts onto the larger needle size.

Work increase rnd:

Size 1: *K7, M1L; rep from * to the end of rnd. 8 sts inc'd. 64 sts total.

Size 2: *K4, M1L; rep from * to the end of the rnd. 16 sts inc'd. 80 sts total.

Size 3: *K9, M1L; rep from * to the end of the rnd. 8 sts inc'd. 80 sts total.

Work rnds 1–30 of Colorwork Chart A (page 83), joining CC1 and CC2 where shown. The chart repeats 4 (5, 5) times around the sock. Cut CC2 after rnd 16. Cut CC1 on completion of chart.

Knit 1 rnd with MC. For Sizes 1 and 3 only, transfer the sts back onto the smaller needle size.

Using MC, work decrease rnd:

Size 1: *K6, K2tog; rep from * to the end of the rnd. 8 sts dec'd. 56 sts total.

Size 2: *K3, K2tog; rep from * to the end of the rnd. 16 sts dec'd. 64 sts total.

Size 3: *K8, K2tog; rep from * to the end of the rnd. 8 sts dec'd. 72 sts total.

Rejoin CC2 and start knitting stripes as follows:

Knit 2 rnds with CC2.

Knit 2 rnds with MC.

Continue knitting stripes for a further 1½ inches (4 cm) or however long you would like the leg of your sock to be. Finish after a MC stripe. Cut CC2.

Eye of Partridge Heel Flap

The eye of partridge heel is worked flat and knit back and forth using the 28 (32, 36) sts on Needle 1 with MC. Needle 2 is holding the 28 (32, 36) sts for the instep. You can remove the marker you placed at the beginning.

Row 1 (RS): *Sl1 st purlwise, K1; repeat from * to the end of the row. Turn.

Row 2 (WS): Sl1 st purlwise, P until the end of the row. Turn.

Row 3 (RS): Sl2 st purlwise, *K1, Sl1; repeat from * until 2 sts before the end of the row, K2. Turn.

Row 4 (WS): Same as Row 2.

Repeat these 4 rows, ending on a purl row after a total of 28 (32, 36) rows. There will be 14 (16, 18) edge sts for you to pick up after the heel turn.

Heel Turn

Continuing to use MC, you will now use short rows to turn your heel.

Row 1 (RS): Sl1, K15 (18, 20), SSK, K1, turn.

Row 2 (WS): Sl1, P5 (7, 7), P2tog, P1, turn.

Row 3 (RS): Sl1, K6 (8, 8), SSK, K1, turn.

Row 4 (WS): Sl1, P7 (9, 9), P2tog, P1, turn.

Continue in this pattern: Sl1, K or P to 1 stitch before the gap created by turning in the previous row, SSK or P2tog to close the gap, K1 or P1, turn. Continue until all stitches have been worked, ending with a purl row on the WS. Turn to the right side; you will now have 16 (20, 22) sts left on Needle 1.

Gusset

You will now be picking up stitches along both sides of your heel flap.

With MC, knit across the heel stitches, placing a BOR stitch marker after 8 (10, 11) sts (the halfway point).

Join CC2, knit to the end of the heel sts, then pick up and Ktbl 14 (16, 18) sts along the edge of the heel flap. Pick up and knit 1 more stitch at the corner between the heel flap and instep to help prevent a hole in the corner. Place a stitch marker here to help show you when to decrease in the next round, or adjust the loop and needles so the heel/gusset sts and instep sts are separated there.

Knit the 28 (32, 36) sts on the instep being held on Needle 2. Place a stitch marker after the instep stitches as well, as you did above.

Pick up 1 stitch in the corner and Ktbl 14 (16, 18) sts along the edge of the heel flap. Knit the first half of the heel to the BOR stitch marker.

You now have a total of 46 (54, 60) heel/gusset sts, 28 (32, 36) instep sts and are knitting all stitches again in the round. 74 (86, 96) total sts.

Gusset Decreases

Rnd 1: Knit to 3 sts before the first stitch marker and K2tog, K1, knit across the instep stitches to the second marker, K1, SSK, knit to the BOR stitch marker. 2 sts dec'd.

Rnd 2: Using MC (to maintain stripe pattern), knit all stitches.

Repeat rnds 1 and 2 (while continuing to alternate the 2-row stripes using MC and CC2) until you have decreased to 28 (32, 36) heel/gusset sts. 28 (32, 36) instep sts remain on Needle 2. There are now 56 (64, 72) sts in total.

Foot

Continue to knit stripes, alternating between MC and CC2 every 2 rnds, until the foot of your sock measures approximately 2 inches (5 cm) before the desired length of your sock, finishing on a stripe with CC2.

For size 1 and 3 only, transfer the sts back onto the larger needle size.

Work increase rnd with MC:

Size 1: *K14, M1L; rep from * to the end of the rnd. 4 sts inc'd. 60 sts total.

Size 2: *K10, M1L; rep from * to 4 sts before the end of the rnd, K4. 6 sts inc'd. 70 sts total.

Size 3: *K9, M1L; rep from * to the end of the rnd. 8 sts inc'd. 80 sts total.

Work rnds 1–6 of Colorwork Chart B (page 83), joining CC1 and 2 where shown. The chart repeats 12 (14, 16) times around the sock.

Cut CC1 and CC2.

For size 1 and 3 only, transfer the sts back onto the smaller needle size.

Work decrease rnd:

Size 1: *K13, K2tog; rep from * to the end of the rnd. 4 sts dec'd. 56 sts total.

Size 2: *K9, K2tog; rep from * to 4 sts before the end of the rnd, K4. 6 sts dec'd. 64 sts total.

Size 3: *K8, K2tog; rep from * to the end of the rnd. 8 sts dec'd. 72 sts total.

With MC, knit all rnds until your sock is 1½ inches (4 cm) from the desired finished length. If you are already at this point, continue to the Toe section.

Toe

Your stitches should now be placed equally on Needles 1 and 2. Needle 1 is holding 28 (32, 36) sts at the bottom of your foot, with 14 (16, 18) sts on either side of the BOR marker. Needle 2 is holding 28 (32, 36) sts at the top of your foot.

Setup rnd: Knit 1 more rnd with MC to the BOR marker.

Rnd 1 (decrease rnd):

   Needle 1: Knit until 3 sts remain, K2tog, K1.

   Needle 2: K1, SSK, knit until 3 sts remain, K2tog, K1.

   Needle 1: K1, SSK, knit to BOR.

   4 sts dec'd.

Rnd 2: Knit all sts.

Repeat rnds 1 and 2 until 20 sts remain on each needle (40 sts in total).

Continue knitting only rnd 1 (dec every rnd) until 10 sts remain on each needle (20 sts in total).

Remove BOR stitch marker. K5 sts to the side of the sock. With 10 sts on each needle, join remaining stitches using Kitchener stitch.

Finishing

Weave in all ends. Soak and block. Repeat instructions for the second sock.

Colorwork Chart A

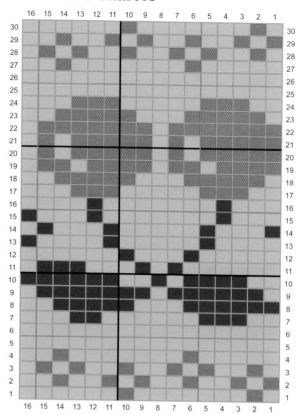

Colorwork Chart B

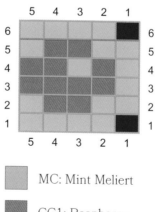

MC: Mint Meliert

CC1: Raspberry

CC2: Teal

Coffee Break

Nothing beats that first comforting sip of hot coffee in the morning. This sock pattern is dedicated to all of us coffee lovers who could not happily go through the day without a coffee break (or two!). Coffee is not only a warm and comforting drink but energy boosting and apparently healthy as well—in moderation, of course! There is something so lovely and simple about the ritual of sitting down with a fresh cup with friends—and, of course, with your latest knitting project to knit a few rows! This pattern creates perfect, cozy socks for all coffee connoisseurs.

Construction Notes

Knit from the top down with a ribbed cuff, this sock includes a colorwork pattern on the leg, with a little simple colorwork decoration before the toe is knitted. These socks are knit with an eye of partridge heel flap and gusset.

Sizing

1 (2, 3)

To fit (foot circumference): 8½ (9½, 10½) inches / 20.5–23 (23.5–25, 26–27.5) cm

Finished circumference: 7½ (8½, 9½) inches / 18–20 (20.5–23, 23.5–25) cm

Recommended ease: Approximately 1 inch (2.5 cm) of negative ease.

Leg/foot length can be easily adjusted. See instructions for details.

Sample shown is knit in size 2 for shoe size US 8.5 (EU 39, UK 6), foot circumference 8¾ inches (22.5 cm).

Materials

Yarn

Fingering weight, GigglingGecko Socklandia Soxs yarn (80% superwash merino wool, 20% nylon), 398 yds (365 m) per 100-g skein.

Shown in

MC: Bantli Brown (1 skein)

CC1: Double Fudge (1 skein)

CC2: Ice Blue (only scrap amounts required)

Any fingering-weight sock yarn can be used for this sock pattern as long as you can obtain the same gauge. A good substitute would be yarn from Hue Loco, Lolabean Yarn Co. or hand-dyed yarn from an indie dyer near you.

Needles

For ribbing and stockinette: US 1 (2.25 mm), 32-inch (80-cm) circular for magic loop, or DPNs, or two circulars or a 9-inch (23-cm) circular needle (as preferred).

For colorwork: US 1.5 (2.5 mm), 32-inch (80-cm) circular for magic loop, or DPNs, or two circulars or a 9-inch (23-cm) circular needle (as preferred).

Important note: *Do check your gauge for fit. Additional sizes can be achieved by going up or down needle sizes.*

Notions

Stitch marker

Scissors

Tapestry needle

Gauge

34 sts x 36 rnds = 4 inches (10 cm) for colorwork.

32 sts x 42 rnds = 4 inches (10 cm) for stockinette and ribbing.

Special Techniques

Knitting Colorwork Socks (page 8)

Kitchener Stitch (page 170)

For all abbreviations, see page 169

Size 3: *K6, M1L; repeat from * to the end of the rnd. 12 sts increased. 84 sts total.

Knit 1 rnd with MC.

Work rnds 1–34 of the colorwork chart (page 88), joining CC1 and CC2 where shown. The chart is worked from right to left, from bottom to the top. The chart is knit 5 (6, 7) times per rnd.

Cut CC1 and CC2.

Knit 1 rnd with MC, transferring the sts back to your US 1 (2.25 mm) needles.

Work decrease rnd:

Size 1: *K13, K2tog; repeat from * to the end of the rnd. 4 sts dec'd. 56 sts total.

Size 2: *K7, K2tog; repeat from * to the end of the rnd. 8 sts dec'd. 64 sts total.

Size 3: *K5, K2tog; repeat from * to the end of the rnd. 12 sts dec'd. 72 sts total.

Knit a further 1¾ inches (4.5 cm) or desired length to heel flap. Cut MC.

Coffee Break Pattern

Cuff

Cast on 56 (64, 72) sts with MC and US 1 (2.25 mm) needle. Divide sts evenly over the two needles and place a marker at the beginning of the round. For DPNs, place half of your sts on one needle and divide the other half over two needles. Be careful when joining in the round not to twist your stitches.

Ribbing Rnd: *K1, P1; rep from * to end of rnd.

Work Ribbing Rnd for a total of 13 rnds, approximately 1¼ inches (3 cm).

Leg

Knit 1 rnd with MC, transferring sts to US 1.5 (2.5 mm) needles (or needle size to achieve gauge in colorwork).

Work increase rnd:

Size 1: *K14, M1L; repeat from * to the end of the rnd. 4 sts increased. 60 sts total.

Size 2: *K8, M1L; repeat from * to the end of the rnd. 8 sts increased. 72 sts total.

Eye of Partridge Heel Flap

The eye of partridge heel is worked flat with the 28 (32, 36) sts on Needle 1 with CC1. Needle 2 is holding the 28 (32, 36) sts for the instep. You can remove the marker you placed at the beginning.

Row 1 (RS): *Sl1 st purlwise, K1; rep from * to the end of the row. Turn.

Row 2 (WS): Sl1 st purlwise, purl to the end of the row. Turn.

Row 3 (RS): Sl2 st purlwise, *K1, Sl1; rep from * to the last 2 sts, K2. Turn.

Row 4 (WS): Same as Row 2.

Repeat these 4 rows ending on a WS (purl) row after a total of 28 (32, 36) rows. There will be 14 (16, 18) edge sts for you to pick up after the heel turn.

Heel Turn

Continuing to use CC1, you will now use short rows to turn your heel.

Row 1 (RS): Sl1, K15 (18, 20), SSK, K1. Turn.

Row 2 (WS): Sl1, P5 (7, 7), P2tog, P1. Turn.

Row 3 (RS): Sl1, K6 (8, 8), SSK, K1. Turn.

Row 4 (WS): Sl1, P7 (9, 9), P2tog, P1. Turn.

Continue in this pattern: Sl1, K or P to 1 stitch before the gap created by turning in the previous row, SSK or P2tog to close the gap, K1 or P1. Turn. (**For size 1 only:** On the last 2 rows you will end with the last SSK or P2tog. There will be no sts remaining to K1 or P1). Continue until all stitches have been worked, ending with a purl row on the WS. Turn to the right side; you will now have 16 (20, 22) sts left on Needle 1.

Gusset

Cut CC1 and rejoin MC.

You will be picking up stitches along both sides of your heel flap.

Knit across the heel stitches, placing a BOR stitch marker after 8 (10, 11) stitches (the halfway point).

Pick up and Ktbl 14 (16, 18) sts along the edge of the heel flap. Pick up and knit 1 more stitch at the corner between the heel flap and instep (to help prevent a hole in the corner). Place a stitch marker here to help show you when to decrease in the next round or adjust the loop and needles so the heel/gusset sts and instep sts are separated there.

Knit the 28 (32, 36) sts on the instep being held on Needle 2. Place a stitch marker after the instep stitches as well, as you did above.

Pick up 1 stitch in the corner and Ktbl 14 (16, 18) sts along the edge of the heel flap. Knit the first half of the heel to the BOR stitch marker.

You now have a total of 46 (54, 60) heel/gusset sts, 28 (32, 36) instep sts and are working all stitches again in the round. 74 (86, 96) sts on your needles in total.

Gusset Decreases

Rnd 1: Knit to 3 sts before the first stitch marker and K2tog, K1, SM. Work across the instep stitches to the second marker, SM, K1, SSK. Knit to the BOR stitch marker. 2 sts dec'd.

Rnd 2: Knit all stitches.

Repeat rnds 1 and 2 until you have decreased to 28 (32, 36) heel/gusset sts. 28 (32, 36) instep sts remain on Needle 2. There are now 56 (64, 72) sts in total.

Foot

With MC continue to knit every rnd until the foot of your sock measures approximately 2 inches (5 cm) less than your desired finished length.

Cut MC.

Change to US 1.5 (2.5 mm) needles.

Work increase rnd with CC1:

Size 1: *K14, M1L; repeat from * to the end of the rnd. 4 sts inc'd. 60 sts total.

Size 2: *K8, M1L; repeat from * to the end of the rnd. 8 sts inc'd. 72 sts total.

Size 3: *K6, M1L; repeat from * to the end of the rnd. 12 sts inc'd. 84 sts total.

Work rnds 1–3 ONLY, of the colorwork chart (page 88), joining CC1 and CC2 where shown. The chart is knit 5 (6, 7) times per rnd.

Cut CC2.

Change to US 1 (2.25 mm) needles.

Work decrease rnd with CC1:

Size 1: *K13, K2tog; repeat from * to the end of the rnd. 4 sts dec'd. 56 sts total.

Size 2: *K7, K2tog; repeat from * to the end of the rnd. 8 sts dec'd. 64 sts total.

Size 3: *K5, K2tog; repeat from * to the end of the rnd. 12 sts dec'd. 72 sts total.

Knit 1 round.

Knit 1 round with CC1.

Toe

Your stitches should now be placed equally on Needles 1 and 2. Needle 1 is holding 28 (32, 36) sts at the bottom of your foot, with 14 (16, 18) sts on either side of the BOR marker. Needle 2 is holding 28 (32, 36) sts at the top of your foot.

Starting from the BOR stitch marker:

Rnd 1 (decrease rnd):

 Needle 1: Knit until 3 sts remain, K2tog, K1.

 Needle 2: K1, SSK, knit until 3 sts remain, K2tog, K1.

 Needle 1: K1, SSK, knit to the BOR stitch marker. 4 sts dec'd.

Rnd 2: Knit all stitches.

Work rnds 1 and 2 until there are 20 sts remaining on each needle (40 sts in total).

Continue working only rnd 1 (dec every rnd) until 10 sts remain on each needle (20 sts in total).

Remove BOR stitch marker. K5 sts to the side of the sock. With 10 sts on each needle, join remaining stitches using Kitchener stitch.

Finishing

Weave in all ends. Soak and block. Repeat instructions for the second sock.

Colorwork Chart

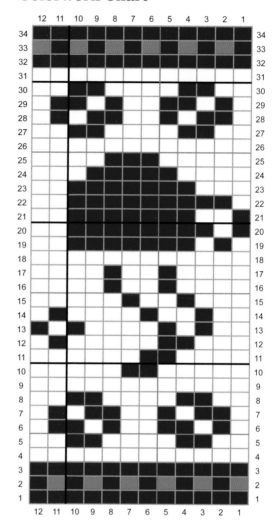

MC: Bantli Brown

CC1: Double Fudge

CC2: Ice Blue

Gelato Socks

These socks are inspired by the warm, sunny, carefree days of summer and trips to the ice cream store to cool down and have a sweet treat. We live a short drive from Italy and are lucky enough to travel there most summers and visit their gelato stores. The big trays of delicious, colorful whipped gelato are a sight to see. This gorgeous hand-dyed yarn from Qing Fibre exudes summery gelato vibes. I wanted to create some sweet socks full of carefree summer memories that can brighten up even a gray rainy day in November.

Construction Notes

Knit from the top down with a twisted ribbed cuff, this sock includes a colorwork pattern on the leg, with a little simple colorwork decoration before the toe is knitted. These socks are knit with a ribbed heel flap and gusset.

Sizing

1 (2, 3)

To fit (foot circumference): 8½ (9½, 10½) inches / 20.5–23 (23.5–25, 26–27.5) cm

Finished circumference: 7½ (8½, 9½) inches / 18–20 (20.5–23, 23.5–25) cm

Recommended ease: Approximately 1 inch (2.5 cm) of negative ease.

Leg/foot length can be easily adjusted. See instructions for details.

Sample shown is knit in size 2 for shoe size US 8.5 (EU 39, UK 6), foot circumference 8¾ inches (22.5 cm).

Materials

Yarn

MC, CC1 and CC4: Fingering weight, Qing Fibre High Twist BFL (100% superwash Bluefaced Leicester wool), 399 yds (365 m) per 100-g skein

CC2 and CC3: Superfine/fingering weight, Lang Yarns Jawoll (75% virgin superwash wool, 25% nylon), 230 yds (210 m) per 50-g skein

Shown in

MC: Jazzy (1 skein)

CC1: Biscuit (20 g)

CC2: Pearl (20 g)

CC3: Rosa (20 g)

CC4: Shusui (20 g)

Any fingering-weight sock yarn can be used for this sock pattern as long as you can obtain the same gauge. A good substitute would be any hand-dyed yarn from an indie dyer near you.

Needles

For ribbing and stockinette: US 1 (2.25 mm), 32-inch (80-cm) circular for magic loop, or DPNs, or two circulars or a 9-inch (23-cm) circular needle (as preferred).

For colorwork: US 1.5 (2.5 mm), 32-inch (80-cm) circular for magic loop, or DPNs, or two circulars or a 9-inch (23-cm) circular needle (as preferred).

Important note: *Do check your gauge for fit. Additional sizes can be achieved by going up or down needle sizes.*

Notions

Stitch marker

Scissors

Tapestry needle

(continued)

Gauge

34 sts x 36 rnds = 4 inches (10 cm) for colorwork.

32 sts x 42 rnds = 4 inches (10 cm) for stockinette and ribbing.

Special Techniques

Knitting Colorwork Socks (page 8)

Kitchener Stitch (page 170)

For all abbreviations, see page 169

Gelato Socks Pattern

Cuff

Cast on 56 (64, 72) sts with MC and US 1 (2.25 mm) needle. Divide sts evenly over the two needles and place a marker at the beginning of the rnd. For DPNs, place half of your sts on one needle and divide the other half over two needles. Join to work in the rnd, being careful not to twist sts.

Ribbing Rnd: *K1tbl, P1; rep from * to end of rnd.

Work Ribbing Rnd for a total of 13 rnds, approximately 1¼ inches (3 cm).

Leg

Knit 1 rnd with MC, transferring sts to US 1.5 (2.5 mm) needles.

Work increase rnd:

Size 1 only: *K14, M1L; repeat from * to the end of the rnd. 4 sts inc'd. 60 sts total.

Size 2 only: *K8, M1L; repeat from * to the end of the rnd. 8 sts inc'd. 72 sts total.

Size 3 only: *K6, M1L; repeat from * to the end of the rnd. 12 sts inc'd. 84 sts total.

Knit 1 rnd with MC.

Work rnds 1–36 of Colorwork Chart A (page 93), joining CC1, CC2 and CC3 where shown. The chart is worked from right to left, from bottom to the top. The chart is knit 5 (6, 7) times per rnd.

Cut CC1, CC2 and CC3.

Knit 1 rnd with MC, transferring sts back to your US 1 (2.25 mm) needles.

Work decrease rnd:

Size 1 only: *K13, K2tog; repeat from * to the end of the rnd. 4 sts dec'd. 56 sts total.

Size 2 only: *K7, K2tog; repeat from * to the end of the rnd. 8 sts dec'd. 64 sts total.

Size 3 only: *K5, K2tog; repeat from * to the end of the rnd. 12 sts dec'd. 72 sts total.

Knit a further 1¾ inches (4.5 cm) or desired length to heel flap. Cut MC.

Heel Flap

The heel is worked flat and knit back and forth using the 28 (32, 36) sts that are currently on Needle 1. Needle 2 is holding the 28 (32, 36) sts for the instep. You can remove the marker you placed at the beginning.

Join CC4.

Row 1 (RS): *Sl1, K1; repeat from * to the end of the row. Turn.

Row 2: (WS): Sl1, purl to the end of the row. Turn.

Repeat these 2 rows, ending on Row 2 (purl row) after a total of 28 (32, 36) rows. There will be 14 (16, 18) edge sts for you to pick up after the heel turn.

Heel Turn

Continuing to use CC4, you will now use short rows to turn your heel.

Row 1 (RS): Sl1, K15 (18, 20), SSK, K1, turn.

Row 2 (WS): Sl1, P5 (7, 7), P2tog, P1, turn.

Row 3 (RS): Sl1, K6 (8, 8), SSK, K1, turn.

Row 4 (WS): Sl1, P7 (9, 9), P2tog, P1, turn.

Continue in this pattern: Sl1, K or P to 1 stitch before the gap created by turning in the previous row, SSK or P2tog to close the gap, K1 or P1, turn. (**For size 1 only:** On the last 2 rows you will end with the last SSK or P2tog. There will be no sts remaining to K1 or P1). Continue until all stitches have been worked, ending with a purl row on the WS. Turn to the right side; you will now have 16 (20, 22) sts left on Needle 1.

Gusset

Cut CC4 and join MC.

You will be picking up stitches along both sides of your heel flap using MC.

Knit across the heel stitches placing a BOR stitch marker after 8 (10, 11) stitches (the halfway point).

Pick up and Ktbl 14 (16, 18) sts along the edge of the heel flap. Pick up and knit 1 more stitch at the corner between the heel flap and instep to help prevent a hole in the corner. Place a stitch marker here to help show you when to decrease in the next round or adjust the loop and needles so the heel/gusset sts and instep sts are separated there.

Work across the 28 (32, 36) instep sts being held on Needle 2. Place a stitch marker after the instep stitches as well, as you did above.

Pick up 1 stitch in the corner and Ktbl 14 (16, 18) along the edge of the heel flap. Knit the first half of the heel to the BOR stitch marker.

You now have a total of 46 (54, 60) heel/gusset sts, 28 (32, 36) instep sts and are working all stitches again in the round. 74 (86, 96) total sts.

Gusset Decreases

Rnd 1: Knit to 3 sts before the first stitch marker and K2tog, K1, knit across the instep stitches to the second marker, K1, SSK. Knit to the BOR stitch marker. 2 sts dec'd.

Rnd 2: Knit all stitches.

Repeat rnds 1 and 2 until you have decreased to 28 (32, 36) heel/gusset sts.

28 (32, 36) instep sts remain on Needle 2. There are now 56 (64, 72) sts in total.

Foot

With MC continue to knit every rnd until the foot of your sock measures approximately 2 inches (5 cm) less than your desired finished length.

Change to US 1.5 (2.5 mm) needles.

> **Size 1 only:** *K14, M1L; repeat from * to the end of the rnd. 4 sts inc'd. 60 sts total.

> **Size 2 only:** *K8, M1L; repeat from * to the end of the rnd. 8 sts inc'd. 72 sts total.

> **Size 3 only:** *K6, M1L; repeat from * to the end of the rnd. 12 sts inc'd. 84 sts total.

Knit 1 rnd with MC.

Work rnds 1–3 of Colorwork Chart B (page 93) joining CC2, CC3 and CC4 where shown. The chart is worked from right to left, bottom to top. The chart is knit 30 (36, 42) times per rnd.

Cut MC, CC2 and CC3.

Change to US 1 (2.25 mm) needles.

Work decrease rnd with CC4:

> **Size 1 only:** *K13, K2tog; repeat from * to the end of the rnd. 4 sts dec'd. 56 sts total.

> **Size 2 only:** *K7, K2tog; repeat from * to the end of the rnd. 8 sts dec'd. 64 sts total.

> **Size 3 only:** *K5, K2tog; repeat from * to the end of the rnd. 12 sts dec'd. 72 sts total.

Knit 1 round.

Toe

Your stitches should now be placed equally on Needles 1 and 2. Needle 1 is holding 28 (32, 36) sts at the bottom of your foot, with 14 (16, 18) sts on either side of the BOR marker. Needle 2 is holding 28 (32, 36) sts at the top of your foot.

Rnd 1 (decrease round):

Needle 1: Knit until 3 sts remain, K2tog, K1.

Needle 2: K1, SSK, knit until 3 sts remain, K2tog, K1.

Needle 1: K1, SSK, knit to the BOR stitch marker.

4 sts dec'd.

Rnd 2: Knit all stitches.

Repeat rnds 1 and 2 until there are 20 sts remaining on each needle (40 sts in total).

Continue working only rnd 1 (dec every rnd) until 10 sts remain on each needle (20 sts in total).

Remove BOR stitch marker. K5 sts to the side of the sock. Join remaining sts using Kitchener stitch.

Finishing

Weave in all ends. Soak and block. Repeat instructions for the second sock.

Colorwork Chart A

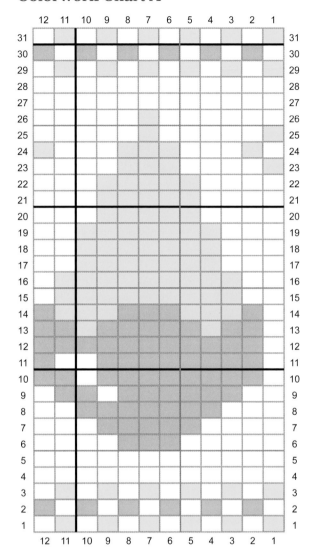

Colorwork Chart B

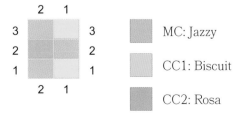

MC: Jazzy

CC1: Biscuit

CC2: Rosa

Spicy Socks

I'm a big spicy food fan and a red chili lover. I couldn't resist creating these socks as a dedication to all things hot. Whether you can handle spicy food or not, these are a very fun and eye-catching pair of socks available to knit in three different sizes. Who doesn't love some fun, bright chilies for their feet? You or your loved ones can enjoy wearing them no matter how delicate your tastebuds are.

Construction Notes

Knit from the top down with a ribbed cuff, this sock includes a chili colorwork pattern throughout the foot, with a little extra simple colorwork decoration by the red-hot toe. These socks are knit with a short row heel.

Sizing

1 (2, 3)

To fit (foot circumference): 8½ (9½, 10½) inches / 20.5–22.5 (23–25.5, 26–27.5) cm

Finished circumference: 7½ (8½, 9½) inches / 18–20 (20.5–23, 23.5–25) cm

Recommended ease: Approximately 1 inch (2.5 cm) of negative ease.

Leg/foot length can be easily adjusted. See instructions for details.

Sample shown is knit in size 2 for shoe size US 8.5 (EU 39, UK 6), foot circumference 8¾ inches (22.5 cm).

Materials

Yarn

Fingering weight, GigglingGecko, Socklandia Soxs yarn (80% superwash merino wool, 20% nylon), 398 yds (365 m) per 100-g skein

Shown in

MC: Midnight (1 skein)

CC1: Jalapeño (1 skein)

CC2: Pomegranate (1 skein)

Any fingering-weight sock yarn can be used for this sock pattern as long as you can obtain the same gauge. A good substitute would be Sweet-Georgia yarns or Madelinetosh.

Needles

For ribbing, heel and toe: US 1 (2.25 mm), 32-inch (80-cm) circular for magic loop, or DPNs, or two circulars or a 9-inch (23-cm) needle (as preferred).

For colorwork: US 1.5 (2.5 mm), 32-inch (80-cm) circular for magic loop, or DPNs, or two circulars or a 9-inch (23-cm) circular needle (as preferred).

Important note: *Do check your gauge for fit. Additional sizes can be achieved by going up or down needle sizes.*

Notions

Stitch marker

Scissors

Tapestry needle

Gauge

34 sts x 38 rnds = 4 inches (10 cm) for colorwork.

36 sts x 44 rnds = 4 inches (10 cm) for ribbing and stockinette.

Special Techniques

Knitting Colorwork Socks (page 8)

Kitchener Stitch (page 170)

For all abbreviations, see page 169

Work rnds 1–40 of Colorwork Chart A (page 99), joining CC1 and CC2 where shown. The chart repeats 5 (6, 7) times around the sock.

Short Row Heel

Using MC, size US 1 (2.25 mm) needle and Needle 1 only, you will now work the heel instructions for your size.

Size 1 only (30 sts on Needle 1):

Row 1 (RS): Sl1, [K12, K2tog] twice, turn work to the WS (leaving 1 st unworked). 2 sts dec'd. There are now 28 sts for the heel in total.

Row 2 (WS): Sl1, P25 (leaving 1 st unworked at the end), turn work to the RS.

Row 3: Sl1, K24 (leaving 2 sts unworked at the end), turn work.

Row 4: Sl1, P23 (1 st before the gap), turn work.

Row 5: Sl1, K22 (1 st before the gap), turn work.

Row 6: Sl1, P21 (1 st before the gap), turn work.

Row 7: Sl1, K to 1 st before the gap, turn work.

Row 8: Sl1, P to 1 st before the gap, turn work.

Repeat Rows 7 and 8 five more times.

Row 19: Sl1, K to 1 st before the gap, turn work.

Row 20: Sl1, P7, turn work.

You should have 8 purl sts in the center and 10 unworked sts on each side.

The heel now needs to be worked back and forth, closing the gaps that have been created from turning the work.

Row 21 (RS): Sl1, K6, SSK (working together 1 st on either side of the gap), M1L, picking up under the SSK st (do not twist the st). Turn work.

Row 22 (WS): Sl1, P7, P2tog, M1Lp, picking up under the P2tog st (do not twist the st), turn work.

Row 23: Sl1, K8, SSK, M1L, turn work.

Row 24: Sl1, P9, P2tog, M1Lp, turn work.

Continue in established pattern for 14 more rows.

Spicy Socks Pattern

Cuff

Cast on 56 (64, 72) sts with MC and US 1 (2.25 mm) needle. Divide sts evenly over the two needles. For DPNs, place half of your sts on one needle and divide the other half over two needles. PM for BOR. Join to work in the rnd, being careful not to twist sts.

Ribbing Rnd: *K2, P2; rep from * to end of rnd.

Work Ribbing Rnd for a total of 12 rnds or approximately 1¼ inches (3 cm).

Leg

With MC and US 1.5 (2.5 mm) needles, or needle size to achieve gauge in colorwork, work increase rnd:

Size 1: *K14, M1L; rep from * to the end of rnd. 4 sts inc'd. 60 sts total.

Size 2: *K8, M1L; rep from * to the end of rnd. 8 sts inc'd. 72 sts total.

Size 3: *K6, M1L, rep from * to the end of rnd. 12 sts inc'd. 84 sts total.

Row 39: (RS): Sl1, K24, SSK, M1L, turn work.

Row 40: (WS): Sl1, P25, P2tog, M1Lp, turn work.

Row 41: (RS): Sl1, [K13, M1L] twice, K1. 2 sts inc'd.

There are now 30 sts on Needle 1.

Continue to the Foot section (page 98).

Size 2 only (36 sts on Needle 1):

Row 1 (RS): Sl1 [K6, K2tog] 4 times, K2, turn work (leaving 1 st unworked). 4 sts dec'd.

There are now 32 sts for the heel in total.

Row 2 (WS): Sl1, P29 (leaving 1 st unworked at the end), turn work to the RS.

Row 3: Sl1, K28 (leaving 2 sts unworked at the end), turn work.

Row 4: Sl1, P27 (1 st before the gap), turn work.

Row 5: Sl1, K26 (1 st before the gap), turn work.

Row 6: Sl1, P25 (1 st before the gap), turn work.

Row 7: Sl1, K to 1 st before the gap, turn work.

Row 8: Sl1, P to 1 st before the gap, turn work.

Work rows 7 and 8 five more times.

Row 19: Sl1, K to 1 st before the gap, turn work.

Row 20: Sl1, P11, turn work.

You should have 12 purl sts in the center and 10 unworked sts on each side.

The heel now needs to be worked back and forth, closing the gaps that have been created from turning the work.

Row 21 (RS): Sl1, K10, SSK (working together 1 st on either side of the gap), M1L, picking up under the SSK (do not twist the st), turn work.

Row 22 (WS): Sl1, P11, P2tog, M1Lp, picking up under the P2tog st (do not twist the st), turn work.

Row 23: Sl1, K12, SSK, M1L, turn work.

Row 24: Sl1, P13, P2tog, M1Lp, turn work.

Continue in established pattern for 14 more rows.

Row 39 (RS): Sl1, K28, SSK, M1L, turn work.

Row 40 (WS): Sl1, P29, P2tog, M1Lp, turn work.

Row 41 (RS): [K8, M1L] 4 times. 4 sts inc'd.

There are now 36 sts on Needle 1.

Continue to the Foot section (page 98).

Size 3 only (42 sts on Needle 1):

Row 1 (RS): Sl1, [K5, K2tog] 5 times, K3, K2tog, turn work to the WS (leaving 1 st unworked). 6 sts dec'd. There are now 36 sts for the heel in total.

Row 2 (WS): Sl1, P33 (leaving 1 st unworked at the end), turn work to the RS.

Row 3: Sl1, K32 (leaving 2 sts unworked at the end), turn work.

Row 4: Sl1, P31 (1 st before the gap), turn work.

Row 5: Sl1, K30 (1 st before the gap), turn work.

Row 6: Sl1, P29 (1 st before the gap), turn work.

Row 7: Sl1, K to 1 st before the gap, turn work.

Row 8: Sl1, P to 1 st before the gap, turn work.

Work rows 7 and 8 six more times.

Foot (All Sizes)

Join back in the round with MC and using the US 1.5 (2.5 mm) needles. You will be working with both Needles 1 and 2 again.

Knit 30 (36, 42) sts on Needle 2 back to the BOR (this will be counted as rnd 1 on Colorwork Chart A).

Rejoin CC1 (and eventually CC2) and resume knitting Colorwork Chart A, starting with rnd 2 and ending on rnd 40. Knit rnds 1–40 once more. Cut CC1.

With MC, knit all rnds until your sock is 2 inches (5 cm) from the desired finished length. If you are already 1½ inches (4 cm) from the desired finished length, skip chart B and start the Toe section.

Work rnds 1–4 of Colorwork Chart B using MC and CC2. The chart repeats 10 (12, 14) times around the sock.

With MC and size US 1.5 (2.25 mm) needles, knit all rnds until your sock is 1½ inches (4 cm) from the desired finished length. If you are already at this point, continue to the Toe section.
Cut MC.

Row 21: Sl1, K to 1 st before the gap, turn work.

Row 22: Sl1, P13, turn work.

You should have 14 purl sts in the center and 11 unworked sts on each side.

The heel now needs to be worked back and forth, closing the gaps that have been created from turning the work.

Row 23 (RS): Sl1, K12, SSK (working together 1 st on either side of the gap). M1L, picking up under the SSK (do not twist the st), turn work.

Row 24 (WS): Sl1, P13, P2tog, M1Lp, picking up under the P2tog st (do not twist the st), turn work.

Row 25: Sl1, K14, SSK, M1L, turn work.

Row 26: Sl1, P15, P2tog, M1Lp, turn work.

Continue in established pattern for 16 more rows.

Row 43 (RS): Sl1, K32, SSK, M1L, turn work.

Row 44 (WS): Sl1, P33, P2tog, M1Lp, turn work.

Row 45 (RS): Sl1, [K5, M1L] 6 times, K5.
6 sts inc'd.

There are now 42 sts on Needle 1.

Toe

Preparation for toe section with CC2:

Size 1: *K13, K2tog; rep from * to end of rnd. 4 sts dec'd. 56 sts in total.

Size 2: *K7, K2tog; rep from * to end of rnd. 8 sts dec'd. 64 sts in total.

Size 3: *K5, K2tog; rep from * to end of rnd. 12 sts dec'd. 72 sts in total.

Your stitches should now be placed equally on Needles 1 and 2. Remove the BOR stitch marker. Needle 1 is holding 28 (32, 36) sts at the bottom of your foot. Needle 2 is holding 28 (32, 36) sts at the top of your foot.

With CC2 and Needle 1, knit 14 (16, 18) sts. Now place the BOR st marker after these sts. This should be in the middle of the sts on Needle 1 at the bottom of your foot.

Setup rnd: Knit 1 more rnd with CC2 to the BOR marker.

Rnd 1 (decrease rnd):

> **Needle 1:** Knit until 3 sts remain, K2tog, K1.
>
> **Needle 2:** K1, SSK, K until 3 sts remain, K2tog, K1.
>
> **Needle 1:** K1, SSK, K to BOR.
>
> 4 sts dec'd.

Rnd 2: Knit all sts.

Repeat rnds 1 and 2 until 20 sts remain on each needle (40 sts in total).

Continue knitting only rnd 1 (dec every rnd) until 10 sts remain on each needle (20 sts in total).

Remove BOR stitch marker. Knit 5 stitches to reach the side of the sock. With 10 sts on each needle, join remaining stitches using Kitchener stitch.

Finishing

Weave in all ends. Soak and block. Repeat instructions for the second sock.

Colorwork Chart B

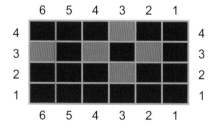

Colorwork Chart A

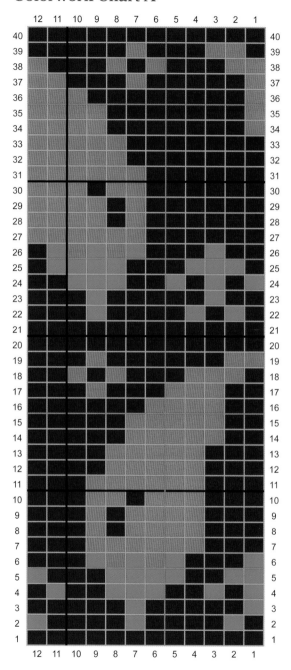

MC: Midnight

CC1: Jalapeño

CC2: Pomegranate

Vitamin C Socks

Mandarin oranges are an excellent source of vitamin C and are a delicious, juicy and healthy snack. A much-welcomed winter fruit, they are often given as a gift at Christmas and seen as a symbol of wealth and prosperity during Lunar New Year celebrations. Here in Switzerland, Samichlaus (or Santa Claus) lives in the forest and brings the well-behaved children bags filled with mandarins, nuts and ginger-bread on December 6. I thought it would be fun to create some socks dedicated to this zesty, bright and possibly lucky fruit!

Construction Notes

Knit from the top down with a twisted ribbed cuff, this sock includes two different mandarin-inspired colorwork patterns, which are worked throughout the leg and foot. These socks are knit with a short row heel.

Sizing

1 (2, 3)

To fit (foot circumference): 8½ (9½, 10½) inches / 20.5–23 (23.5–25, 26–27.5) cm

Finished circumference: 7½ (8½, 9½) inches / 18–20 (20.5–23, 23.5–25) cm

Recommended ease: Approximately 1 inch (2.5 cm) of negative ease.

Leg/foot length can be easily adjusted. See instructions for details.

Sample shown is knit in size 2 for shoe size US 8.5 (EU 39, UK 6), foot circumference 8¾ inches (22.5 cm).

Materials

Yarn

Fingering weight, GigglingGecko Socklandia Soxs (80% superwash merino, 20% nylon), 398 yds (365 m) per 100-g skein

Shown in

MC: Marina Mist (1 skein)

CC1: Mandarin (1 skein)

CC2: Canary (1 skein)

Needles

For ribbing, heel and toe: US 1 (2.25 mm), 32-inch (80-cm) circular for magic loop, or DPNs, or two circulars or a 9-inch (23-cm) circular needle (as preferred).

For colorwork: US 1.5 (2.5 mm), 32-inch (80-cm) circular for magic loop, or DPNs, or two circulars or a 9-inch (23-cm) circular needle (as preferred).

Important note: *Do check your gauge for fit. Additional sizes can be achieved by going up or down needle sizes.*

Notions

Stitch marker

Scissors

Tapestry needle

Gauge

34 sts x 46 rnds = 4 inches (10 cm) for colorwork.

36 sts x 48 rnds = 4 inches (10 cm) for ribbing.

Special Techniques

Knitting Colorwork Socks (page 8)

Kitchener Stitch (page 170)

For all abbreviations, see page 169

Vitamin C Socks Pattern

Cuff

Cast on 56 (64, 72) sts with CC1 and US 1 (2.25 mm) needle. Divide 28 (32, 36) sts evenly over each needle. For DPNs, place half of your sts on one needle and divide the other half over two needles. PM for BOR. Join to work in the rnd being careful not to twist sts.

Ribbing Rnd: *Ktbl, P1; rep from * to end of rnd.

Work Ribbing Rnd for a total of 14 rnds, just over 1¼ inches (3 cm).

Leg

With CC1 and US 1.5 (2.5 mm) needles (or needle size to achieve gauge in colorwork), work increase rnd:

Size 1: *K14, M1L; rep from * to the end of rnd. 4 sts inc'd. 60 sts total.

Size 2: *K8, M1L; rep from * to the end of rnd. 8 sts inc'd. 72 sts total.

Size 3: *K6, M1L, rep from * to the end of rnd. 12 sts inc'd. 84 sts total.

Work rnds 1–27 of Colorwork Chart A (page 105), joining MC and CC2 where shown.

> **Size 1 only:** The chart repeats twice around the sock and then sts 1–12 must be knitted once more.

> **Size 2 only:** The chart repeats 3 times around the sock.

> **Size 3 only:** The chart repeats 3 times around the sock and then sts 1–12 must be knitted once more.

Now work Colorwork Chart B (page 105). This chart repeats 5 (6, 7) times around the sock. Knit rnds 1–20 once and then rnds 1–10 once more. Cut MC and CC2.

Short Row Heel

Using CC1, US 1 (2.25 mm) needle, and Needle 1 only, you will now work the heel instructions for your size.

Size 1 only (30 sts on Needle 1):

Row 1 (RS): Sl1, [K12, K2tog] twice, turn work to the WS (leaving 1 st unworked). 2 sts dec'd. There are now 28 sts for the heel in total.

Row 2 (WS): Sl1, P25 (leaving 1 st unworked at the end), turn work to the RS.

Row 3: Sl1, K24 (leaving 2 sts unworked at the end), turn work.

Row 4: Sl1, P23 (1 st before the gap), turn work.

Row 5: Sl1, K22 (1 st before the gap), turn work.

Row 6: Sl1, P21 (1 st before the gap), turn work.

Row 7: Sl1, K to 1 st before the gap, turn work.

Row 8: Sl1, P to 1 st before the gap, turn work.

Repeat Rows 7 and 8 five more times.

Row 19: Sl1, K to 1 st before the gap, turn work.

Row 20: Sl1, P7, turn work.

You should have 8 purl sts in the center and 10 unworked sts on each side.

The heel now needs to be worked back and forth, closing the gaps that have been created from turning the work.

Row 21 (RS): Sl1, K6, SSK (working together 1 st on either side of the gap), M1L, picking up under the SSK st (do not twist the st). Turn work.

Row 22 (WS): Sl1, P7, P2tog, M1Lp, picking up under the P2tog st (do not twist the st), turn work.

Row 23: Sl1, K8, SSK, M1L, turn work.

Row 24: Sl1, P9, P2tog, M1Lp, turn work.

Continue in established pattern for 14 more rows.

Row 39 (RS): Sl1, K24, SSK, M1L, turn work.

Row 40 (WS): Sl1, P25, P2tog, M1Lp, turn work.

Row 41 (RS): Sl1, [K13, M1L] twice, K1. 2 sts inc'd.

There are now 30 sts on Needle 1.

Continue to the Foot section (page 104).

Size 2 only (36 sts on Needle 1):

Row 1 (RS): Sl1 [K6, K2tog] 4 times. K 2 sts, turn work (leaving 1 st unworked). 4 sts dec'd.

There are now 32 sts for the heel in total.

Row 2 (WS): Sl1, P29 (leaving 1 st unworked at the end), turn work to the RS.

Row 3: Sl1, K28 (leaving 2 sts unworked at the end), turn work.

Row 4: Sl1, P27 (1 st before the gap), turn work.

Row 5: Sl1, K26 (1 st before the gap), turn work.

Row 6: Sl1, P25 (1 st before the gap), turn work.

Row 7: Sl1, K to 1 st before the gap, turn work.

Row 8: Sl1, P to 1 st before the gap, turn work.

Work rows 7 and 8 five more times.

Row 19: Sl1, K to 1 st before the gap, turn work.

Row 20: Sl1, P11, turn work.

You should have 12 purl sts in the center and 10 unworked sts on each side.

The heel now needs to be worked back and forth, closing the gaps that have been created from turning the work.

Row 21 (RS): Sl1, K10, SSK (working together 1 st on either side of the gap), M1L, picking up under the SSK (do not twist the st), turn work.

Row 22 (WS): Sl1, P11, P2tog, M1Lp, picking up under the P2tog st (do not twist the st), turn work.

Row 23: Sl1, K12, SSK, M1L, turn work.

Row 24: Sl1, P13, P2tog, M1Lp, turn work.

Continue in established pattern for 14 more rows.

Row 39 (RS): Sl1, K28, SSK, M1L, turn work.

Row 40 (WS): Sl1, P29, P2tog, M1Lp, turn work.

Row 41 (RS): [K8, M1L] 4 times. 4 sts inc'd.

There are now 36 sts on Needle 1.

Continue to the Foot section (page 104).

Size 3 only (42 sts on Needle 1):

Row 1 (RS): Sl1, [K5, K2tog] 5 times. K3, K2tog, turn work to the WS (leaving 1 st unworked). 6 st dec'd. There are now 36 sts for the heel in total.

Row 2 (WS): Sl1, P33 (leaving 1 st unworked at the end), turn work to the RS.

Row 3: Sl1, K32 (leaving 2 sts unworked at the end), turn work.

Row 4: Sl1, P31 (1 st before the gap), turn work.

Row 5: Sl1, K30 (1 st before the gap), turn work.

Row 6: Sl1, P29 (1 st before the gap), turn work.

Row 7: Sl1, K to 1 st before the gap, turn work.

Row 8: Sl1, P to 1 st before the gap, turn work.

Work rows 7 and 8 six more times.

Row 21: Sl1, K to 1 st before the gap, turn work.

Row 22: Sl1, P13, turn work.

You should have 14 purl sts in the center and 11 unworked sts on each side.

The heel now needs to be worked back and forth, closing the gaps that have been created from turning the work.

Row 23 (RS): Sl1, K12, SSK (working together 1 st on either side of the gap). M1L, picking up under the SSK (do not twist the st), turn work.

Row 24 (WS): Sl1, P13, P2tog, M1Lp, picking up under the P2tog st (do not twist the st), turn work.

Row 25: Sl1, K14, SSK, M1L, turn work.

Row 26: Sl1, P15, P2tog, M1Lp, turn work.

Continue in established pattern for 16 more rows.

Row 43 (RS): Sl1, K32, SSK, M1L, turn work.

Row 44 (WS): Sl1, P33, P2tog, M1Lp, turn work.

Row 45 (RS): Sl1, [K5, M1L] 6 times, K5. 6 sts inc'd.

There are now 42 sts on Needle 1.

Foot (All Sizes)

Join back in the round with MC and US 1.5 (2.5 mm) needles. You will be working with both Needles 1 and 2 again.

Knit 30 (36, 42) sts on Needle 2 back to the BOR (this will be counted as rnd 11 on Colorwork Chart B).

Rejoin CC2 and resume knitting Colorwork Chart B, starting with rnd 12 and ending on rnd 20. Repeat chart B until the foot of your sock is 1½ inches (4 cm) from the desired finished length, ending with a rnd 10 or 20.

Cut CC2. With MC and CC1, work rnds 1 and 2 of Colorwork Chart A. The chart repeats 5 (6, 7) times around the sock.

Knit 1 rnd with CC1.

Cut MC.

Toe

Work decrease rnd with CC1:

Size 1: *K13, K2tog; rep from * to end of rnd. 4 sts dec'd. 56 sts in total.

Size 2: *K7, K2tog; rep from * to end of rnd. 8 sts dec'd. 64 sts in total.

Size 3: *K5, K2tog; rep from * to end of rnd. 12 sts dec'd. 72 sts in total.

Your stitches should now be placed equally on Needles 1 and 2. Remove the BOR stitch marker. Needle 1 is holding 28 (32, 36) sts at the bottom of your foot. Needle 2 is holding 28 (32, 36) sts at the top of your foot.

With CC1 and Needle 1, knit 14 (16, 18) sts. Now place the BOR st marker after these sts. This should be in the middle of the sts on Needle 1 at the bottom of your foot.

Setup rnd: Knit to the BOR marker.

Rnd 1 (decrease rnd):

> **Needle 1:** Knit until 3 sts remain, K2tog, K1.
>
> **Needle 2:** K1, SSK, knit until 3 sts remain, K2tog, K1.
>
> **Needle 1:** K1, SSK, knit to the BOR stitch marker.
>
> 4 sts dec'd.

Rnd 2: Knit all stitches.

Repeat rnds 1 and 2 until 20 sts remain on each needle (40 sts in total).

Continue working only rnd 1 (dec every rnd) until 10 sts remain on each needle (20 sts in total).

Remove BOR stitch marker, then knit 5 stitches to reach the side of the sock. With 10 sts on each needle, join remaining stitches using Kitchener stitch.

Finishing

Weave in all ends. Soak and block. Repeat instructions for the second sock.

Colorwork Chart A

Colorwork Chart B

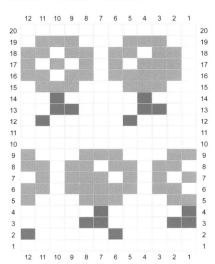

MC: Marina Mist

CC1: Mandarin

CC2: Canary

The Great Outdoors

This section is dedicated to the wonderful scenery here in Switzerland. No matter the time of year, I am always inspired by my time outdoors, whether walking outside in the night or in the forest, hiking up the snowy mountains or relaxing in the garden. I think you will find a pattern that might capture memories of your favorite outdoor adventures too, wherever you are—or help keep your feet warm as you make some new ones!

Summer Meadows

Fragrant meadows full of flowers in the Alps are not only beautiful but very important here in Switzerland. It is believed that these meadows are what makes the cheese and chocolate taste so delicious; the fields are full of gold clover, milchkraut and daisies, which are perfect additions to the alpine cow's diet. On summer hikes, I often find myself running through these meadows pretending to be in The Sound of Music *(while keeping out of the way of any Swiss cows)! I thought I would share this simple pleasure with you and create some socks for any hikes that you might like to go on near meadows where you live. And the great thing about these Summer Meadows socks is that these flowers will always be in bloom and ready for you to wear whatever the time of year. I hope you enjoy watching yours "grow."*

Construction Notes

These socks are knit from the top down, starting with a 2 x 2 ribbed cuff and followed by an easy-to-knit all-over colorwork pattern. Knit with two contrasting colors, this colorwork pattern runs throughout the leg and foot. The heel is constructed as a short row heel, and the rounded toe is completed with Kitchener stitch.

Sizing

1 (2, 3)

To fit (foot circumference): 8½ (9½, 10½) inches / 20.5–23 (23.5–25, 26–27.5) cm

Finished circumference: 7½ (8½, 9½) inches / 18–20 (20.5–23, 23.5–25) cm

Recommended ease: Approximately 1 inch (2.5 cm) of negative ease.

Sample shown is knit in size 2 for shoe size US 8.5 (EU 39, UK 6), foot circumference 8¾ inches (22.5 cm).

Materials

Yarn

Fingering weight, Schwedenrot Yarns High Twist Merino (100% superwash merino wool), 398 yds (365 m) per 100-g skein

Shown in

MC: Ipai (1 skein)

CC: Fluromingo (1 skein)

Any fingering-weight sock yarn can be used for this sock pattern as long as you can obtain the same gauge. A good substitute would be Junkyarn or Neighborhood Fiber Co.

Needles

For ribbing, heel and toe: US 1 (2.25 mm), 32-inch (80-cm) circular for magic loop, or DPNs, or two circulars or a 9-inch (23-cm) needle (as preferred).

For colorwork: US 1.5 (2.5 mm), 32-inch (80-cm) circular for magic loop, or DPNs, or two circulars or a 9-inch (23-cm) circular needle (as preferred).

Important note: *Do check your gauge for fit. Additional sizes can be achieved by going up or down needle sizes.*

Notions

Stitch marker

Scissors

Tapestry needle

Gauge

36 sts x 38 rnds = 4 inches (10 cm) for colorwork.

36 sts x 44 rnds = 4 inches (10 cm) for stockinette and ribbing.

Special Techniques

Knitting Colorwork Socks (page 8)

Kitchener Stitch (page 170)

For all abbreviations, see page 169

Work rnds 1–18 of the colorwork chart (page 112) twice (or as long as you desire the length of the leg to be), joining CC where shown. The chart repeats 5 (6, 7) times around the sock. You can finish on any rnd but do make a note of the last rnd worked, so you can restart on the correct rnd once you have finished the heel.

Short Row Heel

Using MC, size US 1 (2.25 mm) needle and Needle 1 only, you will now work the heel instructions for your size.

Size 1 only (30 sts on Needle 1):

Row 1 (RS): Sl1, [K12, K2tog] twice, turn work to the WS (leaving 1 st unworked). 2 sts dec'd. There are now 28 sts for the heel in total.

Row 2 (WS): Sl1, P25 (leaving 1 st unworked at the end), turn work to the RS.

Row 3: Sl1, K24 (leaving 2 sts unworked at the end), turn work.

Row 4: Sl1, P23 (1 st before the gap), turn work.

Row 5: Sl1, K22 (1 st before the gap), turn work.

Row 6: Sl1, P21 (1 st before the gap), turn work.

Row 7: Sl1, K to 1 st before the gap, turn work.

Row 8: Sl1, P to 1 st before the gap, turn work.

Repeat Rows 7 and 8 five more times.

Row 19: Sl1, K to 1 st before the gap, turn work.

Row 20: Sl1, P7, turn work.

You should have 8 purl sts in the center and 10 unworked sts on each side.

The heel now needs to be worked back and forth, closing the gaps that have been created from turning the work.

Row 21 (RS): Sl1, K6, SSK (working together 1 st on either side of the gap), M1L, picking up under the SSK st (do not twist the st). Turn work.

Row 22 (WS): Sl1, P7, P2tog, M1Lp, picking up under the P2tog st (do not twist the st), turn work.

Row 23: Sl1, K8, SSK, M1L, turn work.

Summer Meadows Pattern

Cuff

Cast on 56 (64, 72) sts with CC and US 1 (2.25 mm) needle. Divide 28 (32, 36) sts evenly over each needle. For DPNs, place half of your sts on one needle and divide the other half over two needles. PM for BOR. Join to work in the rnd, being careful not to twist sts.

Ribbing Rnd: *K2, P2; rep from * to end of rnd.

Change to MC and work Ribbing Rnd for a total of 14 rnds, just over 1¼ inches (3 cm).

Leg

With MC and US 1.5 (2.5 mm) needles, or needle size to achieve gauge in colorwork, work increase rnd:

Size 1: *K14, M1L; rep from * to the end of rnd. 4 sts inc'd. 60 sts total.

Size 2: *K8, M1L; rep from * to the end of rnd. 8 sts inc'd. 72 sts total.

Size 3: *K6, M1L, rep from * to the end of rnd. 12 sts inc'd. 84 sts total.

Row 24: Sl1, P9, P2tog, M1Lp, turn work.

Continue in established pattern for 14 more rows.

Row 39 (RS): Sl1, K24, SSK, M1L, turn work.

Row 40 (WS): Sl1, P25, P2tog, M1Lp, turn work.

Row 41 (RS): Sl1, [K13, M1L] twice, K1. 2 sts inc'd. Turn work.

Row 42 (WS): Sl1, P29.

There are now 30 sts on Needle 1.

Continue to the Foot section (page 112).

Size 2 only (36 sts on Needle 1):

Row 1 (RS): Sl1 [K6, K2tog] 4 times. K2, turn work to WS (leaving 1 st unworked). 4 sts dec'd. There are now 32 sts for the heel in total.

Row 2 (WS): Sl1, P29 (leaving 1 st unworked at the end), turn work to the RS.

Row 3: Sl1, K28 (leaving 2 sts unworked at the end), turn work.

Row 4: Sl1, P27 (1 st before the gap), turn work.

Row 5: Sl1, K26 (1 st before the gap), turn work.

Row 6: Sl1, P25 (1 st before the gap), turn work.

Row 7: Sl1, K to 1 st before the gap, turn work.

Row 8: Sl1, P to 1 st before the gap, turn work.

Work rows 7 and 8 five more times.

Row 19: Sl1, K to 1 st before the gap, turn work.

Row 20: Sl1, P11, turn work.

You should have 12 purl sts in the center and 10 unworked sts on each side.

The heel now needs to be worked back and forth, closing the gaps that have been created from turning the work.

Row 21 (RS): Sl1, K10, SSK (working together 1 st on either side of the gap), M1L, picking up under the SSK (do not twist the st), turn work.

Row 22 (WS): Sl1, P11, P2tog, M1Lp, picking up under the P2tog st (do not twist the st), turn work.

Row 23: Sl1, K12, SSK, M1L, turn work.

Row 24: Sl1, P13, P2tog, M1Lp, turn work.

Continue in established pattern for 14 more rows.

Row 39 (RS): Sl1, K28, SSK, M1L, turn work.

Row 40 (WS): Sl1, P29, P2tog, M1Lp, turn work.

Row 41 (RS): [K8, M1L] 4 times. 4 sts inc'd. Turn work.

Row 42 (WS): Sl1, P35.

There are now 36 sts on Needle 1.

Continue to the Foot section (page 112).

Size 3 only (42 sts on Needle 1):

Row 1 (RS): Sl1, [K5, K2tog] 5 times, K3, K2tog, turn work to the WS (leaving 1 st unworked). 6 sts dec'd. There are now 36 sts for the heel in total.

Row 2 (WS): Sl1, P33 (leaving 1 st unworked at the end), turn work to the RS.

Row 3: Sl1, K32 (leaving 2 sts unworked at the end), turn work.

Row 4: Sl1, P31 (1 st before the gap), turn work.

Row 5: Sl1, K30 (1 st before the gap), turn work.

Row 6: Sl1, P29 (1 st before the gap), turn work.

Row 7: Sl1, K to 1 st before the gap, turn work.

Row 8: Sl1, P to 1 st before the gap, turn work.

Work rows 7 and 8 six more times.

Row 21: Sl1, K to 1 st before the gap, turn work.

Row 22: Sl1, P13, turn work.

You should have 14 purl sts in the center and 11 unworked sts on each side.

The heel now needs to be worked back and forth, closing the gaps that have been created from turning the work.

Row 23 (RS): Sl1, K12, SSK (working together 1 st on either side of the gap), M1L, picking up under the SSK (do not twist the st), turn work.

Row 24 (WS): Sl1, P13, P2tog, M1Lp, picking up under the P2tog st (do not twist the st), turn work.

Row 25: Sl1, K14, SSK, M1L, turn work.

Row 26: Sl1, P15, P2tog, M1Lp, turn work

Continue in established pattern for 16 more rows.

Row 43 (RS): Sl1, K32, SSK, M1L, turn work.

Row 44 (WS): Sl1, P33, P2tog, M1Lp, turn work.

Row 45 (RS): Sl1, [K5, M1L] 6 times, K5. 6 sts inc'd. Turn work.

Row 46 (WS): Sl1, P41.
There are now 42 sts on Needle 1.

Foot (All Sizes)

Join back in the round with MC and CC and US 1.5 (2.5 mm) needle or needle size to achieve gauge in colorwork. Beginning with Needle 1, resume knitting the colorwork chart, beginning where you left off before the heel. Repeat rnds 1–18 until your sock is 1½ inches (4 cm) from the desired finished length.

Cut CC.

Toe

Work decrease rnd with MC:

Size 1: *K13, K2tog; rep from * to end of rnd. 4 sts dec'd. 56 sts in total.

Size 2: *K7, K2tog; rep from * to end of rnd. 8 sts dec'd. 64 sts in total.

Size 3: *K5, K2tog; rep from * to end of rnd. 12 sts dec'd. 72 sts in total.

Your stitches should now be placed equally on Needles 1 and 2. Remove the BOR stitch marker. Needle 1 is holding 28 (32, 36) sts at the bottom of your foot. Needle 2 is holding 28 (32, 36) sts at the top of your foot.

With MC and Needle 1, knit 14 (16, 18) sts. Now place the BOR st marker after these sts. This should be in the middle of the sts on Needle 1 at the bottom of your foot.

Setup rnd: Knit 1 more rnd with MC to the BOR marker.

Rnd 1 (decrease rnd):

Needle 1: Knit until 3 sts remain, K2tog, K1.

Needle 2: K1, SSK, knit until 3 sts remain, K2tog, K1.

Needle 1: K1, SSK, K to BOR.

4 sts dec'd.

Rnd 2: Knit all sts.

Repeat rnds 1 and 2 until 20 sts remain on each needle (40 sts in total).

Continue knitting only rnd 1 (dec every rnd) until 10 sts remain on each needle (20 sts in total).

Remove BOR stitch marker. K5 to the side of the sock. Join remaining sts using Kitchener stitch.

Finishing

Weave in all ends. Soak and block. Repeat instructions for the second sock.

Colorwork Chart

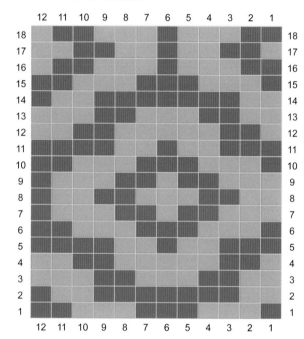

MC: Ipai

CC: Fluromingo

Forest Walk

Spending time mindfully in our local forest is one of my favorite activities. I find it has a calming and peaceful effect and boosts my sense of personal well-being. In Japan, they call this "forest bathing" and it has been part of their holistic preventative healthcare there since 1980. Inspired by the forest paths I often walk here in Switzerland and their beautiful, lush green, orange and brown hues, I wanted to create a thick, warm pair of walking socks—or lounging around home dreaming of the forest socks. Whatever you might prefer!

Construction Notes

These socks are made using thicker-weight, DK sock yarn, so they are quick to make and very warm to wear. They start with an I-cord cast on and continue with a pretty Latvian braid, which is not only decorative but also helps the sock stay up (with the colorwork too), and replaces the need for a ribbing section. With an easy, small and fun colorwork section for the trees, this sock pattern is a quick knit that is suitable even for less experienced sock knitters. The traditional heel flap and gusset is followed by a plain stockinette foot section and ends with a tiny section of colorwork before the toe decreases. This pattern creates a very cozy and warm pair of socks for anyone who is an admirer of the forest.

Sizing

1 (2)

To fit (foot circumference): 8¼–9 (9¼–10¼) inches / 21–23 (24–26) cm

Finished circumference: 7¼–8 (8¼–9¼) inches / 18.5–20.5 (21–24) cm

Recommended ease: Approximately 1 inch (2.5 cm) of negative ease.

Leg/foot length can be easily adjusted. See instructions for details.

Sample shown is knit in size 2 for shoe size US 8.5 (EU 39, UK 6), foot circumference 8¾ inches (22.5 cm).

Materials

Yarn

Light DK-weight yarn, Rowan Felted Tweed (50% wool, 25% viscose, 25% alpaca), 191 yds (175 m) per 50-g skein

Shown in

MC: 161 Avocado 1(2) skeins

CC1: 154 Ginger 1(1) skein

CC2: 145 Treacle 1(1) skein

Any DK-weight sock yarn can be used for this sock pattern as long as you can achieve the same gauge. A good substitute would be KnitPicks® City Tweed DK.

Needles

For stockinette: US 2.5 (3 mm), 32-inch (80-cm) circular for magic loop, or DPNs, or two circulars or a 9-inch (23-cm) circular needle (as preferred).

For colorwork: US 3 (3.25 mm), 32-inch (80-cm) circular for magic loop, or DPNs, or two circulars or a 9-inch (23-cm) circular needle (as preferred).

Important note: *Do check your gauge for fit. Additional sizes can be achieved by going up or down needle sizes.*

Notions

Stitch marker

Scissors

Tapestry needle

(continued)

Gauge

24 sts x 34 rnds = 4 inches (10 cm) for stockinette, on smaller needle.

24 sts x 32 rnds = 4 inches (10 cm) for colorwork, on larger needle.

Special Techniques

I-Cord Cast On (see below)

Latvian Braid (see right)

Knitting Colorwork Socks (page 8)

Kitchener Stitch (page 170)

For all abbreviations, see page 169

Forest Walk Pattern

Cuff

I-Cord Cast On

All sizes, with US 2.5 (3 mm) needle and MC:

Step 1: Cast on 3 sts.

Step 2: Slip them purlwise onto your LH needle. The working yarn is on the left and will now come from the back of your sts.

Step 3: Bring the working yarn across the back of all sts on the LH needle to the first st, and with the RH needle: K1fb, K2. 1 st inc'd. 4 sts total.

Step 4: Slip the last 3 sts purlwise back on to your LH needle (leaving the remaining st on the RH needle).

Step 5: Bring the working yarn across the back of all sts on the LH needle to the first st and with the RH needle: K1fb, K2. 1 st inc'd. 5 sts total.

Step 6: Slip the last 3 sts purlwise back on to your LH needle (leaving the remaining sts on the RH needle).

Continue in this pattern, slipping the last 3 sts purlwise back on to your LH needle and then increasing the first st with the K1fb, until you have created 48 (56) sts in total.

Divide 24 (28) sts evenly over each needle. For DPNs, place half of your sts on one needle and divide the other half over two needles. PM for BOR. Join to work in the rnd, being careful not to twist sts.

Rnd 1: Purl all sts.

Rnd 2: Knit all sts.

Latvian Braid

Using MC and CC1:

Rnd 1: *K1 MC, K1 CC1; rep from * to the end of the rnd.

Bring both yarns to the front of your knitting.

Rnd 2: *P1 MC, P1 CC1; rep from * to end of the rnd. Bring MC under CC and then CC under MC and repeat bringing each strand of yarn under the other, twisting the yarns clockwise, each time.

The yarns will now be twisted. They will untwist on their own in rnd 3.

Rnd 3: *P1 MC, P1 CC1; rep from * to end of the rnd. Bring MC over CC and then CC over MC and repeat bringing each strand of yarn over the other, twisting the yarns counterclockwise each time.

Cut CC1.

Leg

With MC knit 3 rnds.

Work increase rnd:

Size 1: *K24, M1L; rep from * to end of rnd. 2 sts inc'd. 50 sts total.

Size 2: *K14, M1L; rep from * to end of rnd. 4 sts inc'd. 60 sts total.

Changing to the larger US 3 (3.25 mm) needle, knit 1 more rnd. (There are now 5 rnds knitted under the Latvian braid in total.)

Continuing to use the larger needle, work rnds 1–26 of the colorwork chart (page 117), joining CC1 and CC2 where shown. The chart repeats 5 (6) times around the sock.

Using MC, work decrease rnd according to your size:

Work decrease rnd:

Size 1: *K23, K2tog; rep from * to end of rnd. 2 sts dec'd. 48 sts total.

Size 2: *K13, K2tog; rep from * to end of rnd. 4 sts dec'd. 56 sts total.

Using MC and changing back to US 2.5 (3 mm) needles, knit 8 more rnds or 1 inch (2.5 cm) or desired length to heel flap.

Heel Flap

The heel flap is worked flat on the 24 (28) sts on Needle 1 with MC. Needle 2 is holding the 24 (28) sts for the instep. You can remove the BOR marker you placed at the beginning.

Row 1 (RS): Sl1 purlwise, knit to the end of the row. Turn.

Row 2 (WS): Sl1 purlwise, purl to the end of the row. Turn.

Repeat these 2 rows ending on a purl row after a total of 24 (28) rows. There will be 12 (14) edge sts for you to pick up after the heel turn.

Heel Turn

Continuing to use MC, you will now use short rows to turn your heel.

Row 1 (RS): Sl1, K13 (15), SSK, K1, turn.

Row 2 (WS): Sl1, P5 (5), P2tog, P1, turn.

Row 3 (RS): Sl1, K6 (6), SSK, K1, turn.

Row 4 (WS): Sl1, P7 (7), P2tog, P1, turn.

Continue in this pattern: Sl1, K or P to 1 stitch before the gap created by turning in the previous row, SSK or P2tog to close the gap, K1 or P1, turn. Continue until all stitches have been worked, ending with a purl row on the WS. Turn to the right side; you will now have 14 (16) sts left on Needle 2.

Gusset

Using MC, you will be picking up stitches along both sides of your heel flap.

Knit across the heel stitches placing a BOR stitch marker after 7 (8) stitches (the halfway point).

Pick up and Ktbl 12 (14) sts along the edge of the heel flap. Pick up and knit 1 more stitch at the corner between the heel flap and instep to help prevent a hole in the corner. Place a stitch marker here to help show you when to decrease in the next round or adjust the loop and needles so the heel/gusset sts and instep sts are separated there.

Knit the 24 (28) sts on the instep being held on Needle 2. Place a stitch marker after the instep stitches as well, as you did above. Pick up 1 stitch in the corner and Ktbl 12 (14) sts along the edge of the heel flap. Knit the first half of the heel to the BOR stitch marker.

You now have a total of 40 (46) heel/gusset sts, 24 (28) instep sts and are knitting all stitches again in the round. 64 (74) total sts.

Gusset Decreases

Rnd 1: Knit to 3 sts before the first stitch marker and K2tog, K1. Knit across the instep stitches to the second marker, K1, SSK. Knit to the BOR stitch marker. 2 sts dec'd.

Rnd 2: Knit all stitches.

Repeat rnds 1 and 2 until you have decreased to 24 (28) heel/gusset sts. 24 (28) instep sts remain on Needle 2. There are now 48 (56) sts in total.

Foot (All Sizes)

Knit with MC and US 2.5 (3 mm) needles until 2 inches (5 cm) from the beginning of your toe.

Work increase rnd:

Size 1: *K24, M1L; rep from * to end of rnd. 2 sts inc'd. 50 sts total.

Size 2: *K14, M1L; rep from * to end of rnd. 4 sts inc'd. 60 sts total.

Rejoin CC2 and work rnds 1–3 only of the colorwork chart. The chart repeats 5 (6) times around the sock. Cut CC2.

The remainder of the sock is worked with MC.

Work decrease rnd:

Size 1: *K23, K2tog; rep from * to end of rnd. 2 sts dec'd. 48 sts in total.

Size 2: *K13, K2tog; rep from * to end of rnd. 4 sts dec'd. 56 sts in total.

Your sock should now be approximately 1½ inches (4 cm) from your desired length.

Toe

Your stitches should now be placed equally on Needles 1 and 2. Needle 1 is holding 24 (28) sts at the bottom of your foot, with 12 (14) sts on either side of the BOR marker. Needle 2 is holding 24 (28) sts at the top of your foot.

Setup rnd: Knit 1 more rnd with MC to the BOR marker.

Rnd 1 (decrease rnd):

Needle 1: Knit until 3 sts remain, K2tog, K1.

Needle 2: K1, SSK until 3 sts remain, K2tog, K1.

Needle 1: K1, SSK, K to BOR.

4 sts dec'd.

Rnd 2: Knit all sts.

Repeat rnds 1 and 2 until 20 sts remain on each needle (40 sts in total).

Continue working only rnd 1 (dec every rnd) until 10 sts remain on each needle (20 sts in total).

Remove BOR stitch marker. K5 to the side of the sock. Join remaining sts using Kitchener stitch.

Finishing

Weave in all ends. Knit your second sock. Hand-wash gently in cool water, dry flat and enjoy!

Colorwork Chart

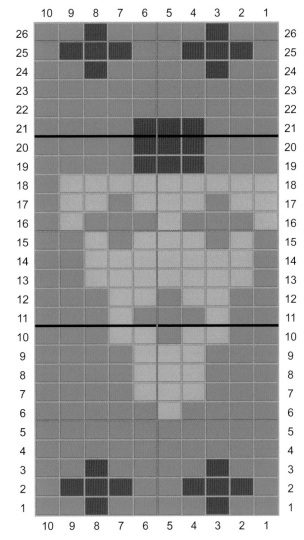

MC: 161 Avocado

CC1: 154 Ginger

CC2: 145 Treacle

Grape Picking

Grape harvests are a very serious subject for wine lovers and are a lot of physical hard work. There is apparently an art to deciding when a grapevine is ready to be picked (mainly determined by taste). Too early or too late, and the crop could be completely ruined. These grapes, however, are much less complicated and can be knit and worn at any time of the year. They are a quick and fun pair of socks to make, and cozy enough to be worn in the evening while maybe sipping on your favorite glass of red!

Construction Notes

Knit from the top down with a ribbed cuff, this sock includes a simple grape colorwork pattern throughout the leg and foot. The heel is constructed as a short row heel.

Sizing

1 (2, 3)

To fit (foot circumference): 7 (8½, 9½) inches / 17–19 (20.5–23, 23.5–25) cm

Finished circumference: 6 (7½, 8½) inches / 14.5–16.5 (18–20, 20.5–23) cm

Recommended ease: Approximately 1 inch (2.5 cm) of negative ease.

Leg/foot length can be easily adjusted. See instructions for details.

Sample shown is knit in size 2 for shoe size US 8.5 (EU 39, UK 6), foot circumference 8¾ inches (22.5 cm).

Materials

Yarn

Fingering weight, Neighborhood Fiber Co. Organic Studio Sock (100% organic merino wool), 398 yds (365 m) per 100-g skein

Shown in

MC: Rosemont (1 skein)

CC1: Remington (1 skein)

CC2: Anacostia (1 skein)

Needles

For ribbing, heel and toe: US 1 (2.25 mm), 32-inch (80-cm) circular for magic loop, or DPNs, or two circulars or a 9-inch (23-cm) circular needle (as preferred).

For colorwork: US 1.5 (2.5 mm), 32-inch (80-cm) circular for magic loop, or DPNs, or two circulars or a 9-inch (23-cm) circular needle (as preferred).

Important note: *Do check your gauge for fit. Additional sizes can be achieved by going up or down needle sizes.*

Notions

Stitch marker

Scissors

Tapestry needle

Gauge

34 sts x 38 rnds = 4 inches (10 cm) for colorwork.

36 sts x 44 rnds = 4 inches (10 cm) for stockinette and ribbing.

Important Note: *Only scrap amounts of yarn are required for the contrast colors for these socks.*

Special Techniques

Knitting Colorwork Socks (page 8)

Kitchener Stitch (page 170)

For all abbreviations, see page 169

Grape Picking Pattern

Cuff

Cast on 56 (64, 72) sts with MC and US 1 (2.25 mm) needle. Divide sts evenly over the two needles. For DPNs, place half of your sts on one needle and divide the other half over two needles. PM for BOR. Be careful when joining in the round not to twist your stitches.

Ribbing Rnd: *K1, P1; rep from * to end of rnd.

Work Ribbing Rnd for a total of 13 rnds, approximately 1¼ inches (3 cm).

Leg

With MC and US 1.5 (2.5 mm) needles, or needle size to achieve gauge in colorwork, work increase rnd:

Size 1: *K14, M1L; rep from * to the end of rnd. 4 sts inc'd. 60 sts total.

Size 2: *K10, M1L; rep from * to the last 4 sts, K4. 6 sts inc'd. 70 sts total.

Size 3: *K9, M1L; rep from * to the end of rnd. 8 sts inc'd. 80 sts total.

Work the colorwork chart (page 122), joining CC1 and CC2 where shown. The chart repeats 6 (7, 8) times around the sock. Work rnds 1–22 once, then work rnds 1–12.

Continue on to the Heel section.

Short Row Heel

Using MC, size US 1 (2.25 mm) needle, and Needle 1 only, you will now work the heel instructions for your size.

Size 1 only (30 sts on Needle 1):

Row 1 (RS): [Sl1, K12, K2tog] twice, turn work to the WS (leaving 1 st unworked). 2 sts decreased. There are now 28 sts on your needles for the heel in total.

Row 2 (WS): Sl1, P25 (leaving 1 st unworked at the end), turn work to the RS.

Row 3: Sl1, K24 (leaving 2 sts unworked at the end), turn work.

Row 4: Sl1, P23 (1 st before the gap), turn work.

Row 5: Sl1, K22 (1 st before the gap), turn work.

Row 6: Sl1, P21 (1 st before the gap), turn work.

Row 7: Sl1, K to 1 st before the gap, turn work.

Row 8: Sl1, P to 1 st before the gap, turn work.

Repeat Rows 7 and 8 five more times.

Row 19: Sl1, K to 1 st before the gap, turn work.

Row 20: Sl1, P7, turn work.

You should have 8 purl sts in the center and 10 unworked sts on each side.

The heel now needs to be worked back and forth, closing the gaps that have been created from turning the work.

Row 21 (RS): Sl1, K6, SSK (working together 1 st on either side of the gap), M1L, picking up under the SSK st (do not twist the st). Turn work.

Row 22 (WS): Sl1, P7, P2tog, M1Lp, picking up under the P2tog st (do not twist the st), turn work.

Row 23: Sl1, K8, SSK, M1L, turn work.

Row 24: Sl1, P9, P2tog, M1Lp, turn work.

Continue in established pattern for 14 more rows.

Row 39 (RS): Sl1, K24, SSK, M1L, turn work.

Row 40 (WS): Sl1, P25, P2tog, M1Lp, turn work.

Row 41 (RS): Sl1, [K13, M1L] twice, K1. 2 sts inc'd.

There are now 30 sts on Needle 1.

Continue to the Foot section (page 121).

Size 2 only (35 sts on Needle 1):

Row 1 (RS): Sl1 [K9, K2tog] 3 times. 3 sts dec'd, turn work to the WS (leaving 1 st unworked). There are now 32 sts on your needles for the heel in total.

Row 2 (WS): Sl1, P29 (leaving 1 st unworked at the end), turn work to the RS.

Row 3: Sl1, K28 (leaving 2 sts unworked at the end), turn work.

Row 4: Sl1, P27 (1 st before the gap), turn work.

Row 5: Sl1, K26 (1 st before the gap), turn work.

Row 6: Sl1, P25 (1 st before the gap), turn work.

Row 7: Sl1, K to 1 st before the gap, turn work.

Row 8: Sl1, P to 1 st before the gap, turn work.

Work rows 7 and 8 five more times.

Row 19: Sl1, K to 1 st before the gap, turn work.

Row 20: Sl1, P11, turn work.

You should have 12 purl sts in the center and 10 unworked sts on each side.

The heel now needs to be worked back and forth, closing the gaps that have been created from turning the work.

Row 21 (RS): Sl1, K10, SSK (working together 1 st on either side of the gap), M1L, picking up under the SSK (do not twist the st), turn work.

Row 22 (WS): Sl1, P11, P2tog, M1Lp, picking up under the P2tog st (do not twist the st), turn work.

Row 23: Sl1, K12, SSK, M1L, turn work.

Row 24: Sl1, P13, P2tog, M1Lp, turn work.

Continue in established pattern for 14 more rows.

Row 39 (RS): Sl1, K28, SSK, M1L, turn work.

Row 40 (WS): Sl1, P29, P2tog, M1Lp, turn work.

Row 41 (RS): [K8, M1L] 4 times. 4 sts inc'd.

There are now 36 sts on Needle 1.

Continue to the Foot section.

Size 3 only (40 sts on Needle 1):

Row 1 (RS): Sl1, [K7, K2tog] 4 times, K2, turn work to the WS (leaving 1 st unworked). 4 sts dec'd. There are now 36 sts for the heel in total.

Row 2 (WS): Sl1, P33 (leaving 1 st unworked at the end), turn work to the RS.

Row 3: Sl1, K32 (leaving 2 sts unworked at the end), turn work.

Row 4: Sl1, P31 (1 st before the gap), turn work.

Row 5: Sl1, K30 (1 st before the gap), turn work.

Row 6: Sl1, P29 (1 st before the gap), turn work.

Row 7: Sl1, K to 1 st before the gap, turn work.

Row 8: Sl1, P to 1 st before the gap, turn work.

Work rows 7 and 8 six more times.

Row 21: Sl1, K to 1 st before the gap, turn work.

Row 22: Sl1, P13, turn work.

You should have 14 purl sts in the center and 11 unworked sts on each side.

The heel now needs to be worked back and forth, closing the gaps that have been created from turning the work.

Row 23 (RS): Sl1, K12, SSK (working together 1 st on either side of the gap). M1L, picking up under the SSK (do not twist the st), turn work.

Row 24 (WS): Sl1, P13, P2tog, M1Lp, picking up under the P2tog st (do not twist the st), turn work.

Row 25: Sl1, K14, SSK, M1L, turn work.

Row 26: Sl1, P15, P2tog, M1Lp, turn work.

Continue in established pattern for 16 more rows.

Row 43 (RS): Sl1, K32, SSK, M1L, turn work.

Row 44 (WS): Sl1, P33, P2tog, M1Lp, turn work.

Row 45 (RS): Sl1, [K8, M1L] 4 times, K to end. 4 sts inc'd.

There are now 40 sts on Needle 1.

Foot (All Sizes)

Join back in the round with MC and using the US 1.5 (2.5 mm) needles. You will be working with both Needles 1 and 2 again.

Knit 30 (35, 40) sts on Needle 2 back to the BOR (this will count as rnd 13 on the colorwork chart).

Continue working the colorwork chart, starting with rnd 14 and ending on rnd 22. Work rnds 1–22 until the sock is approximately 1½ inches (4 cm) from the desired finished length, ending after a rnd 1 or a rnd 11. Cut CC1 and CC2.

Toe

Work decrease rnd with MC:

Size 1: *K13, K2tog; rep from * to end of rnd. 4 sts dec'd. 56 sts in total.

Size 2: *K9, K2tog; rep from * to last 4 sts, K4. 6 sts dec'd. 64 sts in total.

Size 3: *K8, K2tog; rep from * to end of rnd. 8 sts dec'd. 72 sts in total.

Your stitches should now be placed equally on Needles 1 and 2. Remove the BOR stitch marker. Needle 1 is holding 28 (32, 36) sts at the bottom of your foot. Needle 2 is holding 28 (32, 36) sts at the top of your foot.

With MC and Needle 1, knit 14 (16, 18) sts. Now place the BOR st marker after these sts. This should be in the middle of the sts on Needle 1 at the bottom of your foot.

Starting from the BOR stitch marker:

Rnd 1 (decrease round):

    Needle 1: Knit until 3 sts remain, K2tog, K1.

    Needle 2: K1, SSK, knit until 3 sts remain, K2tog, K1.

    Needle 1: K1, SSK, knit to the BOR stitch marker.

    4 sts dec'd.

Rnd 2: Knit all stitches.

Repeat rnds 1 and 2 until 20 sts remain on each needle (40 sts in total).

Continue working only rnd 1 (dec every rnd) until 10 sts remain on each needle (20 sts in total).

Remove BOR stitch marker, then knit 5 stitches to reach the side of the sock. With 10 sts on each needle, join remaining stitches using Kitchener stitch.

Finishing

Weave in all ends. Soak and block. Repeat instructions for the second sock.

Colorwork Chart

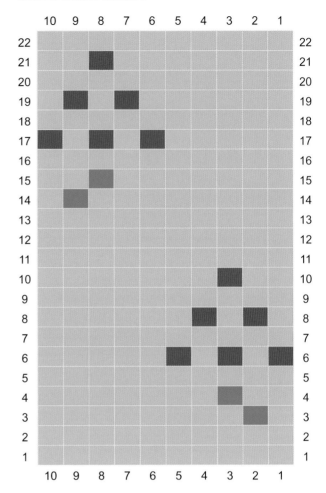

MC: Rosemont

CC1: Remington

CC2: Anacostia

Midnight in Zermatt

The Midnight in Zermatt socks are perfect for wearing while hiking up a mountain, after a day of skiing or for relaxing by a cozy fire with a warm cup of cocoa. These socks are named after the magical village of Zermatt in the Swiss Alps, which famously sits under the majestic Matterhorn mountain. Inspired by the colors of the town in winter, with its dark blue night sky and purple streets below covered in glistening snow, these socks have a simple colorwork motif reminiscent of the mountain peaks.

Construction Notes

Knit from the top down with a ribbed cuff, this sock has a simple graphic colorwork pattern on the leg which is then repeated just before the toe. Knit with three colors, these socks have a ribbed heel flap and gusset.

Sizing

1 (2, 3)

To fit (foot circumference): 8½ (9½, 10½) inches / 20.5–23 (23.5–25, 26–27.5) cm

Finished circumference: 7½ (8½, 9½) inches / 18–20 (20.5–23, 23.5–25) cm

Recommended ease: Approximately 1 inch (2.5 cm) of negative ease.

Leg/foot length can be easily adjusted. See instructions for details.

Sample shown is knit in size 2 for shoe size US 8.5 (EU 39, UK 6), foot circumference 8¾ inches (22.5 cm).

Materials

Yarn

MC and CC2: Fingering weight, GigglingGecko Socklandia Soxs (80% superwash merino wool, 20% nylon), 398 yds (365 m) per 100-g skein

CC1: Fingering weight, Filcolana Arwetta® Classic (80% merino, 20% nylon), 230 yds (210 m) per 50-g skein

Shown in

MC: Snow is Falling (1 skein)

CC1: Lavender Frost (267) (1 skein)

CC2: Midnight (1 skein)

Any fingering-weight sock yarn can be used for this sock pattern as long as you can obtain the same gauge. A good substitute would be KnitPicks Stroll, Lolo Did It Everyday Sock or Coop Knits Socks Yeah!

Needles

For ribbing and stockinette: US 1 (2.25 mm), 32-inch (80-cm) circular for magic loop, or DPNs, or two circulars or a 9-inch (23-cm) needle (as preferred).

For colorwork: US 1.5 (2.5 mm), 32-inch (80-cm) circular for magic loop, or DPNs, or two circulars or a 9-inch (23-cm) needle (as preferred).

Important note: *Do check your gauge for fit. Additional sizes can be achieved by going up or down needle sizes.*

Notions

Stitch marker

Scissors

Tapestry needle

Gauge

36 sts x 38 rnds = 4 inches (10 cm) for colorwork.

36 sts x 44 rnds = 4 inches (10 cm) for stockinette and ribbing.

Special Techniques

Knitting Colorwork Socks (page 8)

Kitchener Stitch (page 170)

For all abbreviations, see page 169

Midnight in Zermatt Pattern

Cuff

Cast on 56 (64, 72) sts with CC1 and US 1 (2.25 mm) needle. Divide sts evenly over the two needles and place a marker at the beginning of the round. For DPNs, place half of your sts on one needle and divide the other half over two needles. Be careful when joining in the round not to twist your stitches.

Ribbing Rnd: *Ktbl, P1; rep from * to end of rnd.

Work Ribbing Rnd for a total of 15 rnds, approximately just over 1 inch (2.5 cm).

Leg

Work increase rnd with CC1 while transferring sts to US 1.5 (2.5 mm) needle.

Size 1: *K14, M1L; repeat from * to the end of the rnd. 4 sts increased. 60 sts total.

Size 2: *K8, M1L; repeat from * to the end of the rnd. 8 sts increased. 72 sts total.

Size 3: *K6, M1L; repeat from * to the end of the rnd. 12 sts increased. 84 sts total.

Work rnds 1–37 of Colorwork Chart A (page 127), joining MC and CC2 where shown. The chart is worked from right to left, from bottom to the top. The chart is knit 5 (6, 7) times per rnd.

Cut CC1 and CC2.

Knit 1 rnd with MC, transferring sts back to your US 1 (2.25 mm) needles.

Work decrease rnd:

Size 1: *K13, K2tog; repeat from * to the end of the rnd. 4 sts dec'd. 56 sts total.

Size 2: *K7, K2tog; repeat from * to the end of the rnd. 8 sts dec'd. 64 sts total.

Size 3: *K5, K2tog; repeat from * to the end of the rnd. 12 sts dec'd. 72 sts total.

Using US 1 (2.25 mm) needle and MC knit a further 1 inch (2.5 cm) (or however long you would like the leg of your sock to be) before starting the heel flap. Cut MC.

Slipped Stitch Heel Flap

The heel is worked flat and knit back and forth using the 28 (32, 36) sts on Needle 1 with CC1. Needle 2 is holding the 28 (32, 36) sts for the instep. You can remove the marker you placed at the beginning of the round.

Row 1 (RS): Sl1 purlwise, *K1, P1; rep from * until there is 1 st remaining, K1. Turn.

Row 2 (WS): Sl1 purlwise, P to the end of row. Turn.

Repeat these 2 rows ending on a purl row after a total of 28 (32, 36) rows. There will be 14 (16, 18) edge sts for you to pick up after the heel turn.

Heel Turn

Continuing to use CC1, you will now use short rows to turn your heel.

Row 1 (RS): Sl1, K15 (18, 20), SSK, K1. Turn.

Row 2 (WS): Sl1, P5 (7, 7), P2tog, P1. Turn.

Row 3 (RS): Sl1, K6 (8, 8), SSK, K1. Turn.

Row 4 (WS): Sl1, P7 (9, 9), P2tog, P1. Turn.

Continue in this pattern: Sl1, K or P to 1 stitch before the gap created by turning in the previous row, SSK or P2tog to close the gap, K1 or P1. Turn. (**For size 1 only:** On the last 2 rows you will end with the last SSK or P2tog. There will be no sts remaining to K1 or P1). Continue until all stitches have been worked, ending with a purl row on the WS. Turn to the right side; you will now have 16 (20, 22) sts left on Needle 1.

Cut CC1.

Gusset

Using MC, you will now be picking up stitches along both sides of your heel flap.

Knit across the heel stitches, placing a BOR stitch marker after 8 (10, 11) sts (the halfway point).

Pick up and Ktbl 14 (16, 18) sts along the edge of the heel flap. Pick up and knit 1 more stitch at the corner between the heel flap and instep to help prevent a hole in the corner. Place a stitch marker here to help show you when to decrease in the next round or adjust the loop and needles so the heel/gusset sts and instep sts are separated there.

Knit the 28 (32, 36) sts on the instep being held on Needle 2. Place a stitch marker after the instep stitches as well, as you did above.

Pick up 1 stitch in the corner and Ktbl 14 (16, 18) sts along the edge of the heel flap. Knit the first half of the heel to the BOR stitch marker.

You now have a total of 46 (54, 60) heel/gusset sts, 28 (32, 36) instep sts and are working all stitches again in the round.

Gusset Decreases

Rnd 1: Knit to 3 sts before the first stitch marker and K2tog, K1, SM. Work across the instep to the second marker, SM, K1, SSK. Knit to the BOR stitch marker.

Rnd 2: Knit all stitches.

Repeat rnds 1 and 2 until you have decreased to 28 (32, 36) heel/gusset sts. 28 (32, 36) instep sts remain on Needle 2. There are now 56 (64, 72) sts in total.

Foot

With MC continue to knit all the sts until the foot of your sock measures approximately 4 inches (10 cm) shorter than your desired overall sock length.

Work increase rnd with MC, while transferring the sts onto your US 1.5 (2.5 mm) needles:

Size 1: *K14, M1L; repeat from * to the end of the rnd. 4 sts inc'd. 60 sts total.

Size 2: *K8, M1L; repeat from * to the end of the rnd. 8 sts inc'd. 72 sts total.

Size 3: *K6, M1L; repeat from * to the end of the rnd. 12 sts inc'd. 84 sts total.

Knit 1 rnd with MC.

Work rnds 1–19 of Colorwork Chart B (page 127), joining CC1 and CC2 where shown. The chart is worked from right to left, bottom to top per rnd. The chart is knit 5 (6, 7) times per rnd.

Cut MC and CC2.

Work decrease rnd with CC1 while transferring back onto the US 1 (2.25 mm) needle:

Size 1: *K13, K2tog; repeat from * to the end of the rnd. 4 sts dec'd. 56 sts total.

Size 2: *K7, K2tog; repeat from * to the end of the rnd. 8 sts dec'd. 64 sts total.

Size 3: *K5, K2tog; repeat from * to the end of the rnd. 12 sts dec'd. 72 sts total.

Using US 1 (2.25 mm) needle and CC1, knit 1 more round before starting the toe.

Toe

Your stitches should now be placed equally on Needles 1 and 2. Needle 1 is holding 28 (32, 36) sts at the bottom of your foot, with 14 (16, 18) sts on either side of the BOR marker. Needle 2 is holding 28 (32, 36) sts at the top of your foot.

Starting from the BOR stitch marker:

Rnd 1 (decrease rnd):

> **Needle 1:** Knit until 3 sts remain, K2tog, K1.

> **Needle 2:** K1, SSK, knit until 3 sts remain, K2tog, K1.

> **Needle 1:** K1, SSK, knit to the BOR stitch marker.

> 4 sts dec'd.

Rnd 2: Knit all stitches.

Repeat rnds 1 and 2 until there are 20 sts remaining on each needle (40 sts in total).

Continue working only rnd 1 (dec every rnd) until 10 sts remain on each needle (20 sts in total).

Remove BOR stitch marker. Knit 5 sts to the side of the sock. With 10 sts on each needle, join remaining stitches using Kitchener stitch.

Finishing

Weave in all ends. Soak and block. Repeat instructions for the second sock.

Colorwork Chart A

Colorwork Chart B

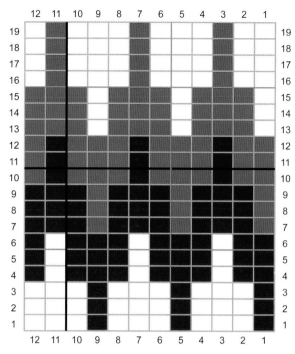

☐ MC: Snow is Falling

▨ CC1: Lavender Frost (267)

■ CC2: Midnight

Starry Night

Inspired by the traditional knitting motifs that can be found in Norway, these Starry Night socks are perfect long socks for wearing on cold wintery nights with skirts or jeans and are guaranteed to keep you snug and warm. The colorwork stars will joyfully peek out over your snow boots. Knitting these long socks will keep you captivated with their easy-to-knit colorwork patterns and stripes that continue all the way down the leg and foot. You'll want to knit "just one more row"!

Construction Notes

These knee-length socks are knitted from the top down with a ribbed cuff, followed by a traditional colorwork star pattern, followed by stripes running throughout the leg and foot. A small detail of colorwork is repeated again before the toe. These socks are knit with a ribbed heel flap and gusset.

Sizing

1 (2, 3)

To fit (foot circumference): 7 (8½, 9¾) inches / 17–19 (20.5–23, 24–26) cm

Finished circumference: 6 (7½, 8¾) inches / 14.5–16.5 (18–20, 26.5–28.5) cm

Finished calf circumference: 10 (11, 13½) inches / 24–26 (27–30, 33–36) cm

Recommended ease: Approximately 1 inch (2.5 cm) of negative ease.

Leg/foot length can be easily adjusted. See instructions for details.

Sample shown is knit in size 2 for shoe size US 8.5 (EU 39, UK 6), foot circumference 8¾ inches (22.5 cm).

Materials

Yarn

Fingering weight, John Arbon Textiles Exmoor Sock 4ply (60% Exmoor Blueface, 20% Corriedale, 10% Zwartbles, 10% nylon), 218 yds (200 m) per 50-g skein

Shown in

MC: Blooth (2 skeins)

CC1: Bell Heather (2 skeins)

CC2: Mackerel-Sky (1 skein)

Any fingering-weight sock yarn can be used for this sock pattern as long as you can obtain the same gauge. A good substitute would be Retrosaria Rosa Pomar Mondim yarn or SweetGeorgia Yarns BFL+Silk Fine.

Needles

For ribbing, stockinette and colorwork on the foot: US 1.5 (2.5 mm), 32-inch (80-cm) circular for magic loop, or DPNs, or two circulars or a 9-inch (23-cm) circular needle (as preferred).

For colorwork on the leg: US 2 (2.75 mm), 32-inch (80-cm) circular for magic loop, or DPNs, or two circulars or a 9-inch (23-cm) circular needle (as preferred).

Important note: *Do check your gauge for fit. Additional sizes can be achieved by going up or down needle sizes.*

Notions

Stitch marker

Scissors

Tapestry needle

(continued)

Gauge

30 sts x 38 rnds = 4 inches (10 cm) for ribbing, stockinette and colorwork on the foot.

28 sts x 36 rnds = 4 inches (10 cm) for colorwork on the leg.

Special Techniques

Knitting Colorwork Socks (page 8)

Jogless Stripes (page 171)

Kitchener Stitch (page 170)

For all abbreviations, see page 169

Starry Night Pattern

Cuff

Cast on 64 (72, 84) sts with MC and US 1.5 (2.5 mm) needles. Divide sts evenly over the two needles and place a marker at the beginning of the round. For DPNs, place half of your sts on one needle and divide the other half over two needles. Be careful when joining in the round not to twist your stitches.

Ribbing Rnd: *K2, P2; rep from * to end of rnd.

Work Ribbing Rnd for a total of 25 rnds, approximately 2¼ inches (6 cm).

Leg

Knit 1 rnd with MC, transferring sts to US 2 (2.75 mm) needles (or needle size to achieve gauge in colorwork).

Work increase:

Size 1: *K10, M1L; rep from * to 4 sts before the end of rnd, K4. 6 sts inc'd. 70 sts total.

Size 2: *K6, M1L; rep from * to the end of the rnd. 12 sts inc'd. 84 sts total.

Size 3: *K6, M1L; rep from * to the end of the rnd. 14 sts inc'd. 98 sts total.

Work rnds 1–43 of Colorwork Chart A (page 133), joining CC1 and CC2 where shown. The chart is worked from right to left, from bottom to the top. The chart repeats 5 (6, 7) times around the sock.

Cut CC2.

Knit 1 rnd with MC, transferring the sts back to your US 1.5 (2.5 mm) needles.

Work decrease rnd:

Size 1: *K9, K2tog; rep from * to 4 sts before the end of the rnd, K4. 6 sts dec'd. 64 sts total.

Size 2: *K5, K2tog; rep from * to the end of the rnd. 12 sts dec'd. 72 sts total.

Size 3: *K5, K2tog; rep from * to the end of the rnd. 14 sts dec'd. 84 sts total.

Knit 2 rnds with MC. You will now have 4 rnds of MC in total since completing Colorwork Chart A.

Start knitting stripes as follows:

Knit 4 rnds with CC1.

Knit 4 rnds with MC.

Repeat these stripes once more.

Knit 1 rnd with CC1.

Using CC1, work decrease rnd:

Size 1: *K6, K2tog; rep from * to the end of the rnd. 8 sts dec'd. 56 sts total.

Size 2: *K7, K2tog; rep from * to the end of the rnd. 8 sts dec'd. 64 sts total.

Size 3: *K5, K2tog; rep from * to the end of the rnd. 12 sts dec'd. 72 sts total.

Knit 2 more rnds with CC1.

Start knitting stripes as follows:

Knit 4 rnds with MC.

Knit 4 rnds with CC1.

Repeat these stripes 5 more times.

Your sock will now be 12¼ inches (31 cm) long. Continue to the Ribbed Heel Flap instructions.

Ribbed Heel Flap

The ribbed heel is worked flat with MC and the 28 (32, 36) sts on Needle 1. Needle 2 is holding the 28 (32, 36) sts for the instep. You can remove the marker you placed at the beginning.

Row 1 (RS): *Sl1 st purlwise, K1; rep from * to the end of the row. Turn.

Row 2 (WS): Sl1 st purlwise, P until the end of the row. Turn.

Repeat these 2 rows, ending on a purl row after a total of 28 (32, 36) rows. There will be 14 (16, 18) edge sts for you to pick up after the heel turn.

Heel Turn

Continuing to use MC, you will now use short rows to turn your heel.

Row 1 (RS): Sl1, K15 (18, 20), SSK, K1. Turn.

Row 2 (WS): Sl1, P5 (7, 7), P2tog, P1. Turn.

Row 3 (RS): Sl1, K6 (8, 8), SSK, K1. Turn.

Row 4 (WS): Sl1, P7 (9, 9), P2tog, P1. Turn.

Continue in this pattern: Sl1, K or P to 1 stitch before the gap created by turning in the previous row, SSK or P2tog to close the gap, K1 or P1. Turn.

(**For size 1 only:** On the last 2 rows you will end with the last SSK or P2tog. There will be no sts remaining to K1 or P1.) Continue until all stitches have been worked, ending with a purl row on the WS. Turn to the right side; you will now have 16 (20, 22) sts left on Needle 1.

Gusset

You will now be picking up stitches along both sides of your heel flap.

With MC, knit across the heel stitches, placing a BOR stitch marker after 8 (10, 11) sts (the halfway point).

Pick up and Ktbl 14 (16, 18) sts along the edge of the heel flap. Pick up and knit 1 more stitch at the corner between the heel flap and instep (to help prevent a hole in the corner). Place a stitch marker here to help show you when to decrease in the next round or adjust the loop and needles so the heel/gusset sts and instep sts are separated there.

Knit the 28 (32, 36) sts on the instep being held on Needle 2. Place a stitch marker after the instep stitches as well, as you did above.

Pick up 1 stitch in the corner and Ktbl 14 (16, 18) sts along the edge of the heel flap. Knit the first half of the heel to the BOR stitch marker.

You now have a total of 46 (54, 60) heel/gusset sts, 28 (32, 36) instep sts and are working all stitches again in the round. 74 (86, 96) sts on your needles in total.

Gusset Decreases

Rnd 1: With MC, knit to 3 sts before the first stitch marker and K2tog, K1, SM. Work across the instep stitches to the second marker, SM, K1, SSK. Knit to the BOR stitch marker. 2 sts dec'd.

Rnd 2: With MC, knit all stitches.

Repeat rnds 1 and 2 (while maintaining the 8-row stripe pattern using MC and CC1) until you have decreased to 28 (32, 36) heel/gusset sts. 28 (32, 36) instep sts remain on Needle 2. There are now 56 (64, 72) sts in total.

Foot (All Sizes)

Continue working the 8-row stripe pattern until the foot of your sock measures approximately 2 inches (5 cm) less than your desired finished length, ending with a MC stripe.

Work increase rnd with CC1:

Size 1: *K8, M1L; rep from * to the end of the rnd. 7 sts inc'd. 63 sts total.

Size 2: *K10, M1L; rep from * to 4 sts before the end of the rnd, K4. 6 sts inc'd. 70 sts total.

Size 3: *K14, M1L; rep from * to 2 sts before the end of the rnd, K2. 5 sts inc'd. 77 sts total.

Work rnds 1–8 of Colorwork Chart B (page 133), using CC1 and rejoining CC2. The chart is knit 9 (10, 11) times per rnd.

Cut CC1 and CC2.

Work decrease rnd with MC:

Size 1: *K7, K2tog; rep from * to the end of the rnd. 7 sts dec'd. 56 sts total.

Size 2: *K9, K2tog; rep from * to 4 sts before the end of the rnd, K4. 6 sts dec'd. 64 sts total.

Size 3: *K13, K2tog; rep from * to 2 sts before the end of the rnd, K2. 5 sts dec'd. 72 sts total.

With MC, knit all rnds until your sock is 1½ inches (4 cm) from your desired finished length. If you are already at this point, continue to the Toe section.

Toe

Your stitches should now be placed equally on Needles 1 and 2. Needle 1 is holding 28 (32, 36) sts at the bottom of your foot, with 14 (16, 18) sts on either side of the BOR marker. Needle 2 is holding 28 (32, 36) sts at the top of your foot.

Setup rnd: Knit all stitches.

Rnd 1 (decrease rnd):

    Needle 1: Knit until 3 sts remain, K2tog, K1.

    Needle 2: K1, SSK, knit until 3 sts remain, K2tog, K1.

    Needle 1: K1, SSK, knit to the BOR stitch marker.

    4 sts dec'd.

Rnd 2: Knit all stitches.

Work rnds 1 and 2 until there are 20 sts remaining on each needle (40 sts in total).

Continue working only rnd 1 (dec every rnd) until 10 sts remain on each needle (20 sts in total).

Remove BOR stitch marker. K5 sts to the side of the sock. With 10 sts on each needle, join remaining stitches using Kitchener stitch.

Finishing

Weave in all ends. Soak and block. Repeat instructions for the second sock.

Colorwork Chart A

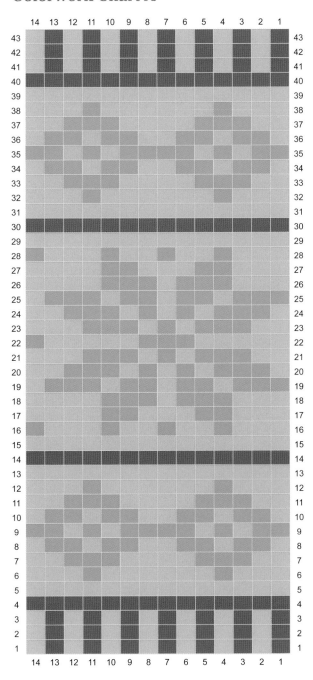

Colorwork Chart B

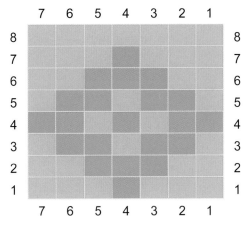

MC: Blooth

CC1: Bell Heather

CC2: Mackerel-Sky

Celebrate Good Times

I love any reason to celebrate, especially the familiarity and tradition of getting ready and preparing for a holiday. And for me, this will also often include knitting a pair of socks to match that season or party. These are great patterns for gifting to friends and family, or just for your enjoyment, for a little moment of fun. Nothing will get you more in the mood for Valentine's, Easter, Halloween or Advent time than casting on a pair of socks to celebrate.

Christmas Eve Skies

There is something so magical about Christmas Eve. The anticipation of waiting for Santa, the excitement of celebrating and the possibility of snow! Whatever age we are, we still search the dark night skies for a glimpse of Santa riding his sleigh or to see if a festive snowfall might appear. These socks are an homage to this much-anticipated time and are a perfect treat for wearing by the Christmas tree or even as a celebratory Christmas Eve knitting cast on.

Construction Notes

Knit from the top down with a ribbed cuff, this sock includes an all-over colorwork pattern of snowflakes (or stars, if you prefer!) in two colors throughout the leg and foot. These socks are knit with a short row heel.

Sizing

1 (2, 3)

To fit (foot circumference): 7 (8½, 9½) inches / 17–19 (20.5–23, 23.5–25) cm

Finished circumference: 6 (7½, 8½) inches / 14.5–16.5 (18–20, 20.5–23) cm

Recommended ease: Approximately 1 inch (2.5 cm) of negative ease.

Leg/foot length can be easily adjusted. See instructions for details.

Sample shown is knit in size 2 for shoe size US 8.5 (EU 39, UK 6), foot circumference 8¾ inches (22.5 cm).

Materials

Yarn

MC: Fingering weight, Filcolana Arwetta Classic (80% merino, 20% nylon), 230 yds (210 m) per 50-g skein

CC: Fingering weight, GigglingGecko Socklandia Soxs (80% merino, 20% nylon), 400 yds (365m) per 100g skein

Shown in

MC: Navy (1 skein)

CC: Snow is Falling (1 skein)

Needles

For ribbing, heel and toe: US 1 (2.25 mm), 32-inch (80-cm) circular for magic loop, or DPNs, or two circulars or a 9-inch (23-cm) circular needle (as preferred).

For colorwork: US 1.5 (2.5 mm), 32-inch (80-cm) circular for magic loop, or DPNs, or two circulars or a 9-inch (23-cm) circular needle (as preferred).

Important note: *Do check your gauge for fit. Additional sizes can be achieved by going up or down needle sizes.*

Notions

Stitch marker

Scissors

Tapestry needle

Gauge

34 sts x 38 rnds = 4 inches (10 cm) for colorwork.

36 sts x 44 rnds = 4 inches (10 cm) for stockinette and ribbing.

Special Techniques

Knitting Colorwork Socks (page 8)

Kitchener Stitch (page 170)

For all abbreviations, see page 169

Christmas Eve Skies Pattern

Cuff

Cast on 56 (64, 72) sts with MC and US 1 (2.25 mm) needle. Divide sts evenly over the two needles. For DPNs, place half of your sts on one needle and divide the other half over two needles. PM for BOR. Join to work in the rnd, being careful not to twist sts.

Ribbing Rnd: *K1tbl, P1; repeat from * to the end of the rnd.

Work Ribbing Rnd for a total of 13 rnds, approximately 1¾ inches (3 cm).

Leg

With MC and needle size US 1.5 (2.5 mm) or needle size to achieve gauge in colorwork, work increase rnd:

Size 1: K3, M1L, [K5, M1L] 10 times, K3, M1L. 12 sts inc'd. 68 sts total.

Size 2: *K8, M1L; rep from * to the end of rnd. 8 sts inc'd. 72 sts total.

Size 3: *K9, M1L; rep from * to the end of rnd. 8 sts inc'd. 80 sts total.

Begin colorwork chart relevant for your size (pages 141–143), joining CC where shown. The size 1 chart is on page 141, the size 2 chart is on page 142 and the size 3 chart is on page 143. The chart repeats twice around the sock.

Work rnds 1–32 once, then work rnds 1–16.

Cut CC. Continue on to the Short Row Heel instructions.

Short Row Heel

Using MC, size US 1 (2.25 mm) needle and Needle 1 only, you will now work the heel instructions for your size.

Size 1 only (34 sts on Needle 1):

Row 1 (RS): Sl1, K1, [K3, K2tog] 6 times, K1, turn work to the WS (leaving 1 st unworked). 6 sts dec'd. There are now 28 sts for the heel in total.

Row 2 (WS): Sl1, P25 (leaving 1 st unworked at the end), turn work to the RS.

Row 3: Sl1, K24 (leaving 2 sts unworked at the end), turn work.

Row 4: Sl1, P23 (1 st before the gap), turn work.

Row 5: Sl1, K22 (1 st before the gap), turn work.

Row 6: Sl1, P21 (1 st before the gap), turn work.

Row 7: Sl1, K to 1 st before the gap, turn work.

Row 8: Sl1, P to 1 st before the gap, turn work.

Repeat Rows 7 and 8 five more times.

Row 19: Sl1, K to 1 st before the gap, turn work.

Row 20: Sl1, P7, turn work.

You should have 8 purl sts in the center and 10 unworked sts on each side.

The heel now needs to be worked back and forth, closing the gaps that have been created from turning the work.

Row 21 (RS): Sl1, K6, SSK (working together 1 st on either side of the gap), M1L, picking up under the SSK st (do not twist the st), turn work.

Row 22 (WS): Sl1, P7, P2tog, M1Lp, picking up under the P2tog st (do not twist the st), turn work.

Row 23: Sl1, K8, SSK, M1L, turn work.

Row 24: Sl1, P9, P2tog, M1Lp, turn work.

Continue in established pattern for 14 more rows.

Row 39 (RS): Sl1, K24, K2tog, M1L, turn work.

Row 40 (WS): Sl1, P25, P2tog, M1Lp, turn work.

Row 41 (RS): Sl1, K1 [K4, M1L] 6 times, K2. 6 sts inc'd. Turn work.

There are now 34 sts on Needle 1.

Row 42 (WS): Sl1, P33.

Continue to the Foot section (page 140).

Size 2 only (36 sts on Needle 1):

Row 1 (RS): Sl1, [K6, K2tog] 4 times, K2, turn work (leaving 1 st unworked). 4 sts dec'd. There are now 32 sts for the heel in total.

Row 2 (WS): Sl1, P29 (leaving 1 st unworked at the end), turn work to the RS.

Row 3: Sl1, K28 (leaving 2 sts unworked at the end), turn work.

Row 4: Sl1, P27 (1 st before the gap), turn work.

Row 5: Sl1, K26 (1 st before the gap), turn work.

Row 6: Sl1, P25 (1 st before the gap), turn work.

Row 7: Sl1, K to 1 st before the gap, turn work.

Row 8: Sl1, P to 1 st before the gap, turn work.

Work rows 7 and 8 five more times.

Row 19: Sl1, K to 1 st before the gap, turn work.

Row 20: Sl1, P11, turn work.

You should have 12 purl sts in the center and 10 unworked sts on each side.

The heel now needs to be worked back and forth, closing the gaps that have been created from turning the work.

Row 21 (RS): Sl1, K10, SSK (working together 1 st on either side of the gap), M1L, picking up under the SSK (do not twist the st), turn work.

Row 22 (WS): Sl1, P11, P2tog, M1Lp, picking up under the P2tog st (do not twist the st), turn work.

Row 23: Sl1, K12, SSK, M1L, turn work.

Row 24: Sl1, P13, P2tog, M1Lp, turn work.

Continue in established pattern for 14 more rows.

Row 39 (RS): Sl1, K28, SSK, M1L, turn work.

Row 40 (WS): Sl1, P29, P2tog, M1Lp, turn work.

Row 41 (RS): [K8, M1L] 4 times. 4 sts inc'd. Turn work.

There are now 36 sts on Needle 1.

Row 42 (WS): Sl1, P35.

Continue to the Foot section (page 140).

Size 3 only (40 sts on Needle 1):

Row 1 (RS): Sl1, [K8, K2tog] 3 times, K6, K2tog, turn work to the WS (leaving 1 st unworked). 4 sts dec'd. There are now 36 sts for the heel in total.

Row 2 (WS): Sl1, P33 (leaving 1 st unworked at the end), turn work to the RS.

Row 3: Sl1, K32 (leaving 2 sts unworked at the end), turn work.

Row 4: Sl1, P31 (1 st before the gap), turn work.

Row 5: Sl1, K30 (1 st before the gap), turn work.

Row 6: Sl1, P29 (1 st before the gap), turn work.

Row 7: Sl1, K to 1 st before the gap, turn work.

Row 8: Sl1, P to 1 st before the gap, turn work.

Work rows 7 and 8 six more times.

Row 21: Sl1, K to 1 st before the gap, turn work.

Row 22: Sl1, P13, turn work.

You should have 14 purl sts in the center and 11 unworked sts on each side.

The heel now needs to be worked back and forth, closing the gaps that have been created from turning the work.

Row 23 (RS): Sl1, K12, SSK (working together 1 st on either side of the gap). M1L, picking up under the SSK (do not twist the st), turn work.

Row 24 (WS): Sl1, P13, P2tog, M1Lp, picking up under the P2tog st (do not twist the st), turn work.

Row 25: Sl1, K14, SSK, M1L, turn work.

Row 26: Sl1, P15, P2tog, M1Lp, turn work.

Continue in established pattern for 16 more rows.

Row 43 (RS): Sl1, K32, SSK, M1L, turn work.

Row 44 (WS): Sl1, P33, P2tog, M1Lp, turn work.

Row 45 (RS): Sl1, [K9, M1L] 3 times. K7, M1L, K1. 4 sts inc'd. Turn work.

There are now 40 sts on Needle 1.

Row 46 (WS): Sl1, P39.

Foot (All Sizes)

Join back in the round with MC and CC and US 1.5 (2.5 mm) needle (or needle size to achieve gauge in colorwork). Beginning with Needle 1, resume knitting the chart relevant to your size, on rnd 17. Continue to repeat the chart until the sock is just over 1 inch (2.5 cm) from the desired length, even if that means ending the colorwork chart before finishing a full repeat.

If you have finished a full repeat and are not at the above length, you may work the decrease rnd below with MC. After working the decrease rnd, knit a few more rnds of stockinette st with MC until you are at the desired length to work the Toe instructions.

Cut CC.

Toe

Work decrease rnd with MC, while transferring your sts onto the US 1 (2.25 mm) needle:

Size 1: K2, K2tog, [K4, K2tog] 10 times, K2, K2tog. 12 sts dec'd. 56 sts in total.

Size 2: *K7, K2tog; rep from * to end of rnd. 8 sts dec'd. 64 sts in total.

Size 3: *K8, K2tog; rep from * to end of rnd. 8 sts dec'd. 72 sts in total.

Your stitches should now be placed equally on Needles 1 and 2; remove the BOR stitch marker. Needle 1 is holding 28 (32, 36) sts at the bottom of your foot. Needle 2 is holding 28 (32, 36) sts at the top of your foot.

With MC and Needle 1, knit 14 (16, 18) sts. Place the BOR st marker after these sts. This should be in the middle of the sts on Needle 1 at the bottom of your foot.

Setup rnd: Knit 1 more rnd with MC to the BOR marker.

Rnd 1 (decrease rnd):

   Needle 1: Knit until 3 sts remain, K2tog, K1.

   Needle 2: K1, SSK, K until 3 sts remain, K2tog, K1.

   Needle 1: K1, SSK, K to BOR.

   4 sts dec'd.

Rnd 2: Knit all sts.

Repeat rnds 1 and 2 until 20 sts remain on each needle (40 sts in total).

Continue knitting only rnd 1 (dec every rnd) until 10 sts remain on each needle (20 sts in total).

Remove BOR stitch marker. Knit 5 stitches to reach the side of the sock. With 10 sts on each needle, join remaining stitches using Kitchener stitch.

Finishing

Weave in all ends. Soak and block. Repeat instructions for the second sock.

Colorwork Chart – Size 1 Only

■ MC: Navy

☐ CC: Snow is Falling

Colorwork Chart – Size 2 Only

■ MC: Navy

□ CC: Snow is Falling

Colorwork Chart – Size 3 Only

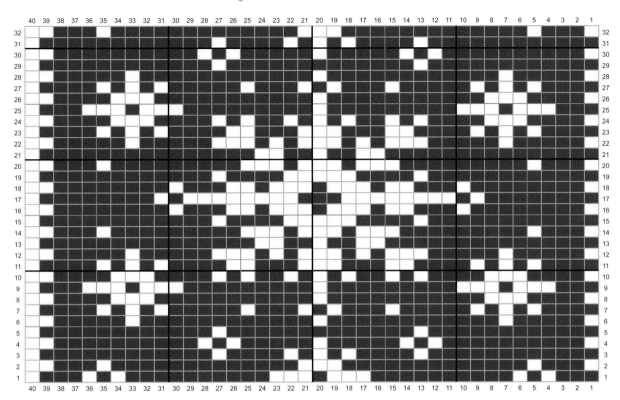

■ MC: Navy

□ CC: Snow is Falling

Eggs for Easter

Eggs are an important part of Easter celebrations, whether they be actual eggs or chocolate ones. I could not resist creating a fun shortie sock dedicated to eggs and the chickens who lay them for us. This is also a perfect sock for any chicken owners out there. My sister is unable to own a cat or a dog because of her partner's allergy to fur, so she rescues chickens instead. She now often has a chicken coming to visit in the evening to sit and watch TV with the family (not advised, they're quite messy!). So, this pattern is dedicated to my sister and her beloved brood of hens.

Construction Notes

This shortie sock (can be adapted for a longer sock too), is knit from the top down with a short twisted-rib cuff. It has a chicken colorwork section which includes some duplicate stitches for the chicken's beak and wattle (a new word for me!). The leg is knit with an easy-to-memorize textured pattern on the foot and has a ribbed heel flap and gusset. The sock is completed with an "egg toe," which is created using a small section of colorwork.

Sizing

1 (2, 3)

To fit (foot circumference): 8 (9, 10) inches / 19.5–21 (21.5–23, 24–26) cm

Finished circumference: 7 (8, 9) inches / 17–19 (19.5–21, 21.5–23) cm

Recommended ease: Approximately 1 inch (2.5 cm) of negative ease.

Leg/foot length can be easily adjusted. See instructions for details.

Sample shown is knit in size 2 for shoe size US 8.5 (EU 39, UK 6), foot circumference 8¾ inches (22.5 cm).

Materials

Yarn

Fingering weight 3-ply yarn, Retrosaria Rosa Pomar Mondim sock yarn (100% non-superwash Portuguese wool), 421 yds (385 m) per 100-g skein

Shown in

MC: 105 Navy (1 skein)

CC1: 100 Natural (1 skein)

CC2: 115 Yellow (1 skein)

CC3: 111 Morango (scrap yarn amount)

Any fingering-weight sock yarn can be used for this sock pattern as long as you can obtain the same gauge. A good substitute would be Knit-Picks Stroll or Filcolana Arwetta Classic.

Needles

For ribbing and stockinette: US 1 (2.25 mm), 32-inch (80-cm) circular for magic loop, or DPNs, or two circulars or a 9-inch (23-cm) circular needle (as preferred).

For colorwork: US 1.5 (2.5 mm), 32-inch (80-cm) circular for magic loop, or DPNs, or two circulars or a 9-inch (23-cm) circular needle (as preferred).

Important note: *Do check your gauge for fit. Additional sizes can be achieved by going up or down needle sizes.*

Notions

Stitch marker

Scissors

Tapestry needle

Gauge

34 sts x 38 rnds = 4 inches (10 cm) for colorwork.

36 sts x 42 rnds = 4 inches (10 cm) for stockinette and ribbing.

(continued)

Special Techniques

Knitting Colorwork Socks (page 8)

Kitchener Stitch (page 170)

Duplicate Stitch (page 170)

For all abbreviations, see page 169

Eggs for Easter Pattern

Cuff

Cast on 56 (64, 72) sts with MC and US 1 (2.25 mm) needle. Divide sts evenly over the two needles and place a marker at the beginning of the rnd. For DPNs, place half of your sts on one needle and divide the other half over two needles. Be careful when joining in the round not to twist your stitches.

Ribbing Rnd: *Ktbl, P1; rep from * to end of rnd.

Work Ribbing Rnd for a total of 9 rnds, approximately ½ inch (1.5 cm).

Leg

Knit 1 rnd with MC, transferring sts to US 1.5 (2.5 mm) needles (or needle size to achieve gauge in colorwork).

Work increase rnd:

Size 1: *K14, M1L; rep from * to the end of rnd. 4 sts inc'd. 60 sts total.

Size 2: *K8, M1L; rep from * to the end of rnd. 8 sts inc'd. 72 sts total.

Size 3: *K6, M1L; rep from * to the end of rnd. 12 sts inc'd. 84 sts total.

Work rnds 1–14 of Colorwork Chart A (page 149), joining CC1 and CC2 where shown. The chart is worked 5 (6, 7) times per rnd. See Special Techniques (page 170) for tips on how to duplicate stitch the hen's beak and wattle, which you will do once the sock has been completed and you have blocked your sock.

Knit 1 rnd with MC, transferring sts back to your US 1 (2.25 mm) needles.

Work decrease rnd:

Size 1: *K13, K2tog; rep from * to end of rnd. 4 sts dec'd. 56 sts in total.

Size 2: *K7, K2tog; rep from * to end of rnd. 8 sts dec'd. 64 sts in total.

Size 3: *K5, K2tog; rep from * to end of rnd. 12 sts dec'd. 72 sts in total.

Continue on to the Slipped Stitch Heel instructions. (For a longer sock, continue knitting rnds of stockinette with your MC until the leg of the sock is as long as you like. Do take note of how many rnds you knit, so both your socks match!).

Slipped Stitch Heel

The heel is worked flat and knit back and forth using the 28 (32, 36) sts on Needle 1 with MC. Needle 2 is holding the 28 (32, 36) sts for the instep. You can remove the marker you placed at the beginning.

Row 1 (RS): Sl1 st purlwise, *K1, P1; rep from * until there is 1 st remaining, K1. Turn.

Row 2 (WS): Sl1 st purlwise, purl to the end of row. Turn.

Repeat these 2 rows, ending on a WS (purl) row after a total of 28 (32, 36) rows. There will be 14 (16, 18) edge sts for you to pick up after the heel turn.

Heel Turn

Continuing to use MC, you will now use short rows to turn your heel.

Row 1 (RS): Sl1, K15 (18, 20), SSK, K1. Turn.

Row 2 (WS): Sl1, P5 (7, 7), P2tog, P1. Turn.

Row 3 (RS): Sl1, K6 (8, 8), SSK, K1. Turn.

Row 4 (WS): Sl1, P7 (9, 9), P2tog, P1. Turn.

Continue in this pattern: Sl1, K or P to 1 stitch before the gap created by turning in the previous row, SSK or P2tog to close the gap, K1 or P1. Turn. **(For size 1 only:** On the last 2 rows you will end with the last SSK or P2tog. There will be no sts remaining to K1 or P1). Continue until all stitches have been worked, ending with a purl row on the WS. Turn to the right side; you will now have 16 (20, 22) sts left on Needle 1.

Gusset

Using MC, you will now be picking up stitches along both sides of your heel flap.

Knit across the heel stitches, placing a BOR stitch marker after 8 (10, 11) sts (the halfway point).

Pick up and Ktbl 14 (16, 18) sts along the edge of the heel flap. Pick up and knit 1 more stitch at the corner between the heel flap and instep to help prevent a hole in the corner. Place a stitch marker here to help show you when to decrease in the next round or adjust the loop and needles so the heel/gusset sts and instep sts are separated there.

Work the 28 (32, 36) sts on the instep being held on Needle 2 beginning with rnd 1 of the Texture Pattern for your size (to the right and on the next page). Place a stitch marker after the instep stitches as well, as you did above.

Pick up 1 stitch in the corner and Ktbl 14 (16, 18) sts along the edge of the heel flap. Knit the first half of the heel to the BOR stitch marker.

You now have a total of 46 (54, 60) heel/gusset sts, 28 (32, 36) instep sts and are working all stitches again in the round.

Gusset Decreases

Rnd 1: Knit up to 3 sts before the first stitch marker and K2tog, K1, SM. Work across the instep, following the next round of the Texture Pattern (see below and on the next page) to the second marker, SM, K1, SSK. Knit to the BOR stitch marker. 2 sts dec'd.

Rnd 2: Work all stitches, following the Texture Pattern for your size on Needle 2.

Repeat rnds 1 and 2 until you have decreased to 28 (32, 36) heel/gusset sts. 28 (32, 36) instep sts remain on Needle 2. There are now 56 (64, 72) sts in total.

Texture Pattern

Size 1 only

Rnd 1:

> **Needle 2 (instep sts):** K4, P1, *K5, P1; rep from * 3 times, K5.

> **Needle 1 (bottom of the foot sts):** K28.

Rnd 2:

> **Needles 2 and 1:** Knit all sts.

Repeat rnds 1 and 2.

Size 2 only

Rnd 1:

> **Needle 2 (instep sts):** K3, P1, *K5, P1; rep from * 4 times, K4.

> **Needle 1 (bottom of the foot sts):** K32.

Rnd 2:

> **Needles 2 and 1:** Knit all sts.

Repeat rnds 1 and 2.

Size 3 only

Rnd 1:

> **Needle 2 (instep sts):** *K5, P1; rep from * 5 times, K6.

> **Needle 1 (bottom of the foot sts):** K36.

Rnd 2:

> **Needles 2 and 1:** Knit all sts.

Repeat rnds 1 and 2.

Foot

With MC continue to work rnds 1 and 2 of the Texture Pattern for your size until the foot of your sock measures just over 2 inches (5.5 cm) shorter than your desired overall sock length.

Work increase rnd with MC, while transferring the sts onto your US 1.5 (2.5 mm) needles:

> **Size 1 only:** *K14, M1L; repeat from * to the end of the rnd. 4 sts inc'd. 60 sts total.

> **Size 2 only:** *K8, M1L; repeat from * to the end of the rnd. 8 sts inc'd. 72 sts total.

> **Size 3 only:** *K6, M1L; repeat from * to the end of the rnd. 12 sts inc'd. 84 sts total.

Work rnds 1–6 of Colorwork Chart B (page 149), joining CC1 where shown. The chart is knit 5 (6, 7) times per rnd.

Cut MC.

Work decrease rnd with CC1 while transferring back onto the US 1 (2.25 mm) needle:

> **Size 1 only:** *K13, K2tog; repeat from * to the end of the rnd. 4 sts dec'd. 56 sts total.

> **Size 2 only:** *K7, K2tog; repeat from * to the end of the rnd. 8 sts dec'd. 64 sts total.

> **Size 3 only:** *K5, K2tog; repeat from * to the end of the rnd. 12 sts dec'd. 72 sts total.

Using the US 1 (2.25 mm) needle and CC1, knit 1 more rnd before starting the Toe section.

Toe

Your stitches should now be placed equally on Needles 1 and 2. Needle 1 is holding 28 (32, 36) sts at the bottom of your foot, with 14 (16, 18) sts on either side of the BOR marker. Needle 2 is holding 28 (32, 36) sts at the top of your foot.

Starting from the BOR stitch marker:

Rnd 1 (decrease round):

> **Needle 1:** Knit until 3 sts remain, K2tog, K1.

> **Needle 2:** K1, SSK, knit until 3 sts remain, K2tog, K1.

> **Needle 1:** K1, SSK, knit to the BOR stitch marker.

> 4 sts dec'd.

Rnd 2: Knit all stitches.

Work rnds 1 and 2 (2 [3, 5]) times in total with CC1. 48 (52, 52) sts. Cut CC1.

Now with CC2, repeat rnds 1 and 2 until there are 20 sts remaining on each needle (40 sts in total).

Continue working only rnd 1 (dec every rnd) until 10 sts remain on each needle (20 sts in total).

Remove BOR stitch marker. K5 sts to the side of the sock. With 10 sts on each needle, join remaining stitches using Kitchener stitch.

Finishing

Weave in all ends. Soak and block and don't forget to add your duplicate stitch beak and wattle! Repeat instructions for the second sock.

Colorwork Chart A

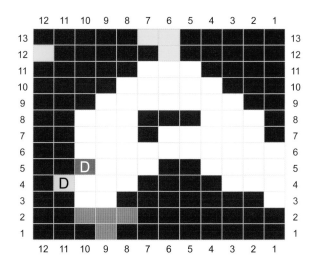

MC: 105 Navy

CC1: 100 Natural

CC2: 115 Yellow

CC3: 111 Morango

D Red Duplicate Stitch

D Yellow Duplicate Stitch

Colorwork Chart B

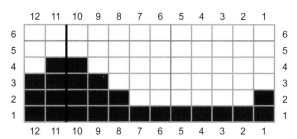

I Heart Socks

I wanted to celebrate Valentine's Day by making some cheerful and bright heart socks. With high expectations for gifts, romantic dinners and sweet gestures, this day can sometimes be met with disappointment and have people feeling left out. I think we should show love all year round to our loved ones, whether it be a kind message, a delicious home-cooked meal or even better, a warm pair of hand-knit socks! And why not show some self-love and make a gorgeous pair of these socks for ourselves, too? With this fun heart design, I couldn't help but name these I Heart Socks. Because to be honest, I do!

Construction Notes

Knit from the top down with a ribbed cuff, this sock includes a simple heart colorwork pattern throughout the leg and foot. These socks are knit with a short row heel.

Sizing

1 (2, 3)

To fit (foot circumference): 7 (8½, 9½) inches / 17–19 (20.5–23, 23.5–25) cm

Finished circumference: 6 (7½, 8½) inches / 14.5–16.5 (18–20, 20.5-23) cm

Recommended ease: Approximately 1 inch (2.5 cm) of negative ease.

Foot length can be easily adjusted. See instructions for details.

Sample shown is knit in size 2 for shoe size US 8.5 (EU 39, UK 6), foot circumference 8¾ inches (22.5 cm).

Materials

Yarn

MC: Fingering weight, Lana Grossa Meilenweit 100 Tweed (80% wool, 20% nylon), 460 yds (420 m) per 100-g skein

CC: Fingering weight, Filcolana Arwetta Classic (80% merino wool, 20% nylon), 230 yds (230 m) per 50-g skein

Shown in

MC: Rosa (1 skein)

CC: Cayenne (1 skein)

Needles

For ribbing, heel and toe: US 1 (2.25 mm), 32-inch (80-cm) circular for magic loop, or DPNs, or two circulars or a 9-inch (23-cm) circular needle (as preferred).

For colorwork: US 1.5 (2.5 mm), 32-inch (80-cm) circular for magic loop, or DPNs, or two circulars or a 9-inch (23-cm) circular needle (as preferred).

Important note: *Do check your gauge for fit. Additional sizes can be achieved by going up or down needle sizes.*

Notions

Stitch marker

Scissors

Tapestry needle

Gauge

34 sts x 38 rnds = 4 inches (10 cm) for colorwork.

36 sts x 44 rnds = 4 inches (10 cm) for stockinette and ribbing.

Special Techniques

Knitting Colorwork Socks (page 8)

Kitchener Stitch (page 170)

For all abbreviations, see page 169

I Heart Socks Pattern

Cuff

Cast on 56 (64, 72) sts with MC and US 1 (2.25 mm) needle. Divide sts evenly over the two needles and place a marker at the beginning of the round. For DPNs, place half of your sts on one needle and divide the other half over two needles. Join to work in the rnd, being careful not to twist sts.

Ribbing Rnd: *K2tbl, P2; repeat from * to the end of the rnd.

Work Ribbing Rnd for a total of 13 rnds, approximately 1 inch (2.5 cm).

Leg

With MC and US 1.5 (2.5 mm) needle (or needle size to achieve gauge in colorwork), work following rnd:

Size 1: Knit all sts.

Size 2: K7, M1L, *K10, M1L; rep from * to 7 sts before the end of the rnd, K7. 6 sts inc'd. 70 sts total.

Size 3: *K6, M1L; rep from * to the end of rnd. 12 sts inc'd. 84 sts total.

Start working the colorwork chart (page 154), joining CC where shown. The chart repeats 4 (5, 6) times around the sock. Knit rnds 1–18 twice and then rnds 1–16. Continue on to work the Short Row Heel section.

Short Row Heel

Using MC, size US 1 (2.25 mm) needles and Needle 1 only, you will now work the heel instructions for your size.

Size 1 only (28 sts on Needle 1):

Row 1 (RS): Sl1, K26 sts, turn work to the WS (leaving 1 st unworked).

Row 2 (WS): Sl1, P25 (leaving 1 st unworked at the end), turn work to the RS.

Row 3: Sl1, K24 (leaving 2 sts unworked at the end), turn work.

Row 4: Sl1, P23 (1 st before the gap), turn work.

Row 5: Sl1, K22 (1 st before the gap), turn work.

Row 6: Sl1, P21 (1 st before the gap), turn work.

Row 7: Sl1, K to 1 st before the gap, turn work.

Row 8: Sl1, P to 1 st before the gap, turn work.

Repeat Rows 7 and 8 five more times.

Row 19: Sl1, K to 1 st before the gap, turn work.

Row 20: Sl1, P7, turn work.

You should have 8 purl sts in the center and 10 unworked sts on each side.

The heel now needs to be worked back and forth, closing the gaps that have been created from turning the work.

Row 21 (RS): Sl1, K6, SSK (working together 1 st on either side of the gap), M1L, picking up under the SSK st (do not twist the st). Turn work.

Row 22 (WS): Sl1, P7, P2tog, M1Lp, picking up under the P2tog st (do not twist the st), turn work.

Row 23: Sl1, K8, SSK, M1L, turn work.

Row 24: Sl1, P9, P2tog, M1Lp, turn work.

Continue in established pattern for 14 more rows.

Row 39 (RS): Sl1, K24, SSK, M1L, turn work.

Row 40 (WS): Sl1, P25, P2tog, M1Lp, turn work.

Row 41 (RS): Sl1, K27.

Row 42 (WS): Sl1, P to end of row, turn work.

There are 28 sts on Needle 1.

Continue to the Foot section (page 154).

Size 2 only (35 sts on Needle 1):

Row 1 (RS): Sl1 [K9, K2tog] 3 times, turn work to the WS (leaving 1 st unworked). 3 sts dec'd. There are now 32 sts for the heel in total.

Row 2 (WS): Sl1, P29 (leaving 1 st unworked at the end), turn work to the RS.

Row 3: Sl1, K28 (leaving 2 sts unworked at the end), turn work.

Row 4: Sl1, P27 (1 st before the gap), turn work.

Row 5: Sl1, K26 (1 st before the gap), turn work.

Row 6: Sl1, P25 (1 st before the gap), turn work.

Row 7: Sl1, K to 1 st before the gap, turn work.

Row 8: Sl1, P to 1 st before the gap, turn work

Work rows 7 and 8 five more times.

Row 19: Sl1, K to 1 st before the gap, turn work.

Row 20: Sl1, P11, turn work.

You should have 12 purl sts in the center and 10 unworked sts on each side.

The heel now needs to be worked back and forth, closing the gaps that have been created from turning the work.

Row 21 (RS): Sl1, K10, SSK (working together 1 st on either side of the gap), M1L, picking up under the SSK (do not twist the st), turn work.

Row 22 (WS): Sl1, P11, P2tog, M1Lp picking up under the P2tog st (do not twist the st), turn work.

Row 23: Sl1, K12, SSK, M1L, turn work.

Row 24: Sl1, P13, P2tog, M1Lp, turn work.

Continue in established pattern for 14 more rows.

Row 39 (RS): Sl1, K28, SSK, M1L, turn work.

Row 40 (WS): Sl1, P29, P2tog, M1Lp, turn work.

Row 41 (RS): Sl1, [K10, M1L] 3 times, K1. 3 sts inc'd. Turn work.

Row 42 (WS): Sl1, P to end of row, turn work.

There are now 35 sts on Needle 1.

Continue to the Foot section (page 154).

Size 3 only (42 sts on Needle 1):

Row 1 (RS): Sl1, [K5, K2tog] 5 times, K3, K2tog, turn work to the WS (leaving 1 st unworked). 6 sts dec'd. There are now 36 sts for the heel in total.

Row 2 (WS): Sl1, P33 (leaving 1 st unworked at the end), turn work to the RS.

Row 3: Sl1, K32 (leaving 2 sts unworked at the end), turn work.

Row 4: Sl1, P31 (1 st before the gap), turn work.

Row 5: Sl1, K30 (1 st before the gap), turn work.

Row 6: Sl1, P29 (1 st before the gap), turn work.

Row 7: Sl1, K to 1 st before the gap, turn work.

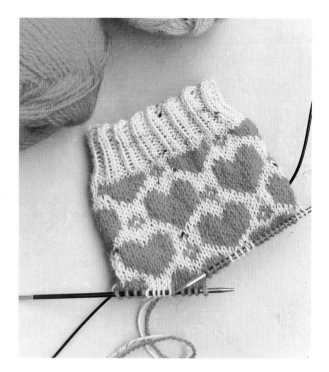

Row 8: Sl1, P to 1 st before the gap, turn work.

Work rows 7 and 8 six more times.

Row 21: Sl1, K to 1 st before the gap, turn work.

Row 22: Sl1, P13, turn work.

You should have 14 purl sts in the center and 11 unworked sts on each side.

The heel now needs to be worked back and forth, closing the gaps that have been created from turning the work.

Row 23 (RS): Sl1, K12, SSK (working together 1 st on either side of the gap). M1L, picking up under the SSK (do not twist the st), turn work.

Row 24 (WS): Sl1, P13, P2tog, M1Lp, picking up under the P2tog st (do not twist the st), turn work.

Row 25: Sl1, K14, SSK, M1L, turn work.

Row 26: Sl1, P15, P2tog, M1Lp, turn work.

Continue in established pattern for 16 more rows.

Row 43 (RS): Sl1, K32, SSK, M1L, turn work.

Row 44 (WS): Sl1, P33, P2tog, M1Lp, turn work.

Row 45 (RS): Sl1, [K6, M1L] 5 times, K4, M1L, K1. 6 sts inc'd. Turn work.

Row 46 (WS): Sl1, P to end of row, turn work.

There are now 42 sts on Needle 1.

Foot (All Sizes)

Join back in the round with MC and CC and US 1.5 (2.5 mm) needle (or needle size to achieve gauge in colorwork). Beginning with Needle 1, resume knitting the colorwork chart, starting with rnd 17. Continue to repeat the chart until the sock is approximately 1½ inches (4 cm) from the desired finished length. You can stop on any rnd.

Cut CC.

Toe

With MC, work this rnd while transferring your sts onto the smaller needle size.

Size 1: Knit all sts.

Size 2: K6, K2tog, *K9, K2tog; rep from * until 7 sts before the end of the rnd, K7. 6 sts dec'd. 64 sts total.

Size 3: *K5, K2tog: rep from * to end of rnd. 12 sts dec'd. 72 sts total.

Your stitches should now be placed equally on Needles 1 and 2. Remove the BOR stitch marker. Needle 1 is holding 28 (32, 36) sts at the bottom of your foot. Needle 2 is holding 28 (32, 36) sts at the top of your foot.

With MC and Needle 1, knit 14 (16, 18) sts. Place the BOR st marker after these sts. This should be in the middle of the sts on Needle 1 at the bottom of your foot.

Starting from the BOR stitch marker

Rnd 1 (decrease rnd):

   Needle 1: Knit until 3 sts remain, K2tog, K1.

   Needle 2: K1, SSK, knit until 3 sts remain, K2tog, K1.

   Needle 1: K1, SSK, knit to the BOR stitch marker.

   4 sts dec'd.

Rnd 2: Knit all stitches.

Repeat rnds 1 and 2 until there are 20 sts remaining on each needle (40 sts in total).

Continue working only rnd 1 (dec every rnd) until 10 sts remain on each needle (20 sts in total).

Remove BOR stitch marker. Knit 5 stitches to reach the side of the sock. With 10 sts on each needle, join remaining stitches using Kitchener stitch.

Finishing

Weave in all ends. Soak and block. Repeat instructions for the second sock.

Colorwork Chart

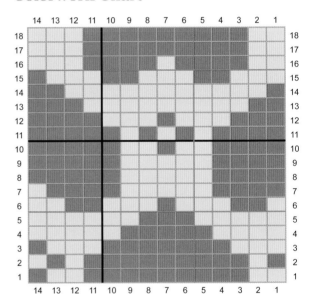

MC: Rosa

CC: Cayenne

I'm Batty for Halloween

I'm a Scorpio and I have always been a bit obsessed (perhaps batty!) with all things Halloween, even when the holiday was only just starting to become popular in the UK when I was a child. One of my most terrifying memories of Halloween was waking up and finding that a bat had flown into my bedroom in the night. On further investigation, I have found out it either meant there was a ghost in the house (not reassuring), bad luck was coming, good luck was coming or we had mice and the bat was hungry. Anyway, my father rescued it and that memory has stuck with me ever since. My appreciation of bats, however, has grown, leading me to design a fun holiday sock featuring their shape in honor of Halloween.

Construction Notes

Knit from the top down with a ribbed cuff, this sock includes a simple bat colorwork pattern throughout the leg and foot. These socks are knit with a contrasting short row heel and toe.

Sizing

1 (2, 3)

To fit (foot circumference): 8 (10, 11) inches / 19.5–21 (24–26, 27–30) cm

Finished circumference: 7 (9, 10) inches / 17–19 (21.5–23, 24–26) cm

Recommended ease: Approximately 1 inch (2.5 cm) of negative ease.

Leg/foot length can be easily adjusted. See instructions for details.

Sample shown is knit in size 2 for shoe size US 8.5 (EU 39, UK 6), foot circumference 8¾ inches (22.5 cm).

Materials

Yarn

Fingering weight, Malabrigo Sock (100% superwash merino), 440 yds (402 m) per 100-g skein

Shown in

MC: Terracotta (1 skein)

CC: Black (1 skein)

Needles

US 1 (2.25 mm), 32-inch (80-cm) circular for magic loop, or DPNs, or two circulars or a 9-inch (23-cm) circular needle (as preferred).

Important note: *Do check your gauge for fit. Additional sizes can be achieved by going up or down needle sizes.*

Notions

Stitch marker

Scissors

Tapestry needle

Gauge

36 sts x 44 rnds = 4 inches (10 cm).

Special Techniques

Knitting Colorwork Socks (page 8)

Kitchener Stitch (page 170)

For all abbreviations, see page 169

I'm Batty for Halloween Pattern

Cuff

Cast on 56 (64, 72) sts with MC and US 1 (2.25 mm) needle. Divide sts evenly over the two needles. For DPNs, place half of your sts on one needle and divide the other half over two needles. PM for BOR. Be careful when joining in the round not to twist your stitches.

Ribbing Rnd: *K1, P1; rep from * to end of rnd.

Work Ribbing Rnd for a total of 13 rnds, approximately 1 inch (2.5 cm).

Leg

Work increase rnd:

Size 1: *K7, M1L; rep from * to end of rnd. 8 sts inc'd. 64 sts total.

Size 2: *K4, M1L; rep from * to end of rnd. 16 sts inc'd. 80 sts total.

Size 3: *K3, M1L; rep from * to end of rnd. 24 sts inc'd. 96 sts total.

Work rnds 1–22 of the colorwork chart (page 159), joining CC where shown. The chart is worked 4 (5, 6) times per rnd. Repeat rnds 1–22 twice (or for desired length of leg), ending on a rnd 11 or 22. Cut MC.

Short Row Heel

Using CC and Needle 1 only, you will now work the heel instructions for your size.

Size 1 only (32 sts on Needle 1):

Row 1 (RS): Sl1, [K5, K2tog] 4 times to 3 sts before the end of the rnd, K2, turn work to the WS (leaving 1 st unworked). 4 sts dec'd. There are now 28 sts for the heel in total.

Row 2 (WS): Sl1, P25 (leaving 1 st unworked at the end), turn work to the RS.

Row 3: Sl1, K24 (leaving 2 sts unworked at the end), turn work.

Row 4: Sl1, P23 (1 st before the gap), turn work.

Row 5: Sl1, K22 (1 st before the gap), turn work.

Row 6: Sl1, P21 (1 st before the gap), turn work.

Row 7: Sl1, K to 1 st before the gap, turn work.

Row 8: Sl1, P to 1 st before the gap, turn work.

Repeat Rows 7 and 8 five more times.

Row 19: Sl1, K to 1 st before the gap, turn work.

Row 20: Sl1, P7, turn work.

You should have 8 purl sts in the center and 10 unworked sts on each side.

The heel now needs to be worked back and forth, closing the gaps that have been created from turning the work.

Row 21 (RS): Sl1, K6, SSK (working together 1 st on either side of the gap), M1L, picking up under the SSK (do not twist the st). Turn work.

Row 22 (WS): Sl1, P7, P2tog, M1Lp, picking up under the P2tog st (do not twist the st), turn work.

Row 23: Sl1, K8, SSK, M1L, turn work.

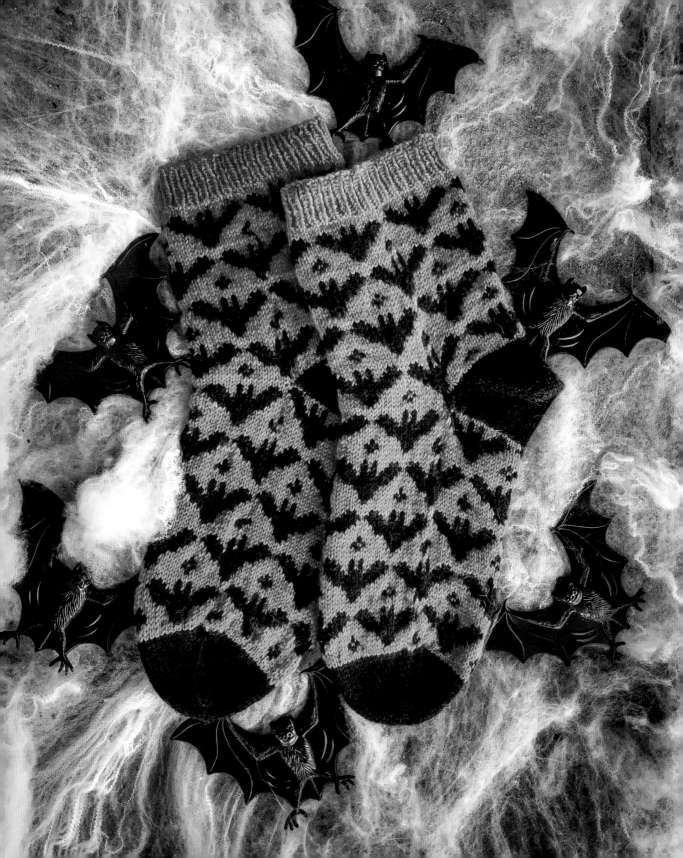

Row 24: Sl1, P9, P2tog, M1Lp, turn work.

Continue in established pattern for 14 more rows.

Row 39 (RS): Sl1, K24, SSK, M1L, turn work.

Row 40 (WS): Sl1, P25, P2tog, M1Lp, turn work.

Row 41 (RS): Sl1, [K6, M1L] 4 times, K3. 4 sts inc'd.

There are now 32 sts on Needle 1.

Continue to the Foot section.

Size 2 only (40 sts on Needle 1):

Row 1 (RS): Sl1, K2, K2tog, [K3, K2tog] 6 times, K2, K2tog, turn work (leaving 1 st unworked). 8 sts dec'd. There are now 32 sts for the heel in total.

Row 2 (WS): Sl1, P29 (leaving 1 st unworked at the end), turn work to the RS.

Row 3: Sl1, K28 (leaving 2 sts unworked at the end), turn work.

Row 4: Sl1, P27 (1 st before the gap), turn work.

Row 5: Sl1, K26 (1 st before the gap), turn work.

Row 6: Sl1, P25 (1 st before the gap), turn work.

Row 7: Sl1, K to 1 st before the gap, turn work.

Row 8: Sl1, P to 1 st before the gap, turn work.

Work rows 7 and 8 five more times.

Row 19: Sl1, K to 1 st before the gap, turn work.

Row 20: Sl1, P11, turn work.

You should have 12 purl sts in the center and 10 unworked sts on each side.

The heel now needs to be worked back and forth, closing the gaps that have been created from turning the work.

Row 21 (RS): Sl1, K10, SSK (working together 1 st on either side of the gap), M1L, picking up under the SSK (do not twist the st), turn work.

Row 22 (WS): Sl1, P11, P2tog, M1Lp, picking up under the P2tog st (do not twist the st), turn work.

Row 23: Sl1, K12, SSK, M1L, turn work.

Row 24: Sl1, P13, P2tog, M1Lp, turn work.

Continue in established pattern for 14 more rows.

Row 39 (RS): Sl1, K28, SSK, M1L, turn work.

Row 40 (WS): Sl1, P29, P2tog, M1Lp, turn work.

Row 41 (RS): Sl1, K3, M1L, [K4, M1L] 7 times. 8 sts inc'd.

There are now 40 sts on Needle 1.

Continue to the Foot section.

Size 3 only (48 sts on Needle 1):

Row 1 (RS): Sl1, *K2, K2tog; rep from * 11 times, K2tog, turn work to the WS (leaving 1 st unworked). 12 sts dec'd. There are now 36 sts for the heel in total.

Row 2 (WS): Sl1, P33 (leaving 1 st unworked at the end), turn work to the RS.

Row 3: Sl1, K32 (leaving 2 sts unworked at the end), turn work.

Row 4: Sl1, P31 (1 st before the gap), turn work.

Row 5: Sl1, K30 (1 st before the gap), turn work.

Row 6: Sl1, P29 (1 st before the gap), turn work.

Row 7: Sl1, K to 1 st before the gap, turn work.

Row 8: Sl1, P to 1 st before the gap, turn work.

Work rows 7 and 8 six more times.

Row 21: Sl1, K to 1 st before the gap, turn work.

Row 22: Sl1, P13, turn work.

You should have 14 purl sts in the center and 11 unworked sts on each side.

The heel now needs to be worked back and forth, closing the gaps that have been created from turning the work.

Row 23 (RS): Sl1, K12, SSK (working together 1 st on either side of the gap), M1L, picking up under the SSK (do not twist the st), turn work.

Row 24 (WS): Sl1, P13, P2tog, M1Lp, picking up under the P2tog st (do not twist the st), turn work.

Row 25: Sl1, K14, SSK, M1L, turn work.

Row 26: Sl1, P15, P2tog, M1Lp, turn work.

Continue in established pattern for 16 more rows.

Row 43 (RS): Sl1, K32, SSK, M1L, turn work.

Row 44 (WS): Sl1, P33, P2tog, M1Lp, turn work.

Row 45 (RS): Sl1, *K3, M1L; rep from * 11 times, K2, M1L. 12 sts inc'd.

There are now 48 sts on Needle 1.

Foot (All Sizes)

Join back in the round with MC. You will be working with both Needles 1 and 2 again.

Knit 32 (40, 48) sts on Needle 2 back to the BOR (this will be counted as either a rnd 12 or rnd 1 on the colorwork chart, depending on where you left off before the heel).

Continue to repeat the chart using MC and CC until your sock is 1½ inches (4 cm) from the desired finished length. Try to finish on a rnd 10 or 21.

Toe

Work decrease rnd:

Size 1: *K6, K2tog; rep from * to end of rnd. 8 sts dec'd. 56 sts in total.

Size 2: *K3, K2tog; rep from * to end of rnd. 16 sts dec'd. 64 sts in total.

Size 3: *K2, K2tog; rep from * to end of rnd. 24 sts dec'd. 72 sts in total.

Your stitches should now be placed equally on Needles 1 and 2; remove the BOR stitch marker. Needle 1 is holding 28 (32, 36) sts at the bottom of your foot. Needle 2 is holding 28 (32, 36) sts at the top of your foot.

With CC and Needle 1, knit 14 (16, 18) sts. Now place the BOR st marker after these sts. This should be in the middle of the sts on Needle 1 at the bottom of your foot.

Setup rnd: Knit 1 rnd with CC to the BOR marker.

Rnd 1 (decrease round):

   Needle 1: Knit until 3 sts remain, K2tog, K1.

   Needle 2: K1, SSK, knit until 3 sts remain, K2tog, K1.

   Needle 1: K1, SSK, knit to the BOR stitch marker.

4 sts dec'd.

Rnd 2: Knit all stitches.

Repeat rnds 1 and 2 until 20 sts remain on each needle (40 sts in total).

Continue knitting only rnd 1 (dec every rnd) until 10 sts remain on each needle (20 sts in total).

Remove BOR stitch marker, then knit 5 stitches to reach the side of the sock. With 10 sts on each needle, join remaining stitches using Kitchener stitch.

Finishing

Weave in all ends. Soak and block. Repeat instructions for the second sock.

Colorwork Chart

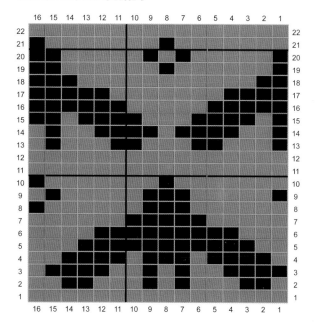

MC: Terracotta

CC: Black

The Holly and the Ivy

I have always loved the excitement of Advent time, and this love grew when we moved to Switzerland. The counting down of the Christmas days leads to every village decorating their streets and lighting up the nights. Christmas markets appear, serving mulled wine (Glühwein), hot chocolate (heisse Schoggi) and many delicious sweet treats. I love seeing houses decorated with natural greenery from the forest, including wreaths and garlands made from pine trees, holly and ivy. And then I am reminded of the "Holly and the Ivy" carol from my British childhood and feel I need a pair of Advent socks to be worn during this magical time.

Construction Notes

Knit from the top down with a ribbed cuff, these socks include a simple decorative colorwork pattern throughout the leg and the foot to represent the Advent garland decorations topped with holly berry bobbles. The holly berry bobbles are replaced with a simple colorwork motif at the bottom of the foot for comfort (we should maybe avoid treading on holly!). These socks are knit with a short row heel.

Sizing

1 (2, 3)

To fit (foot circumference): 7 (8½, 9½) inches / 17–19 (20.5–23, 23.5–25) cm

Finished circumference: 6 (7½, 8½) inches / 14.5–16.5 (18–20, 20.5-23) cm

Recommended ease: Approximately 1 inch (2.5 cm) of negative ease.

Leg/foot length can be easily adjusted. See instructions for details.

Sample shown is knit in size 2 for shoe size US 8.5 (EU 39, UK 6), foot circumference 8¾ inches (22.5 cm).

Materials

Yarn

Fingering weight, Yarn Love Cinderella Fingering (80% superwash BFL wool, 20% nylon), 185 yds (170 m) per 50-g skein

Shown in

MC: Champagne (2 skeins)

CC1: Say Cabernet (1 skein)

CC2: Conifer (1 skein)

Needles

For ribbing, heel and toe: US 1 (2.25 mm), 32-inch (80-cm) circular for magic loop, or DPNs, or two circulars or a 9-inch (23-cm) circular needle (as preferred).

For colorwork: US 1.5 (2.5 mm), 32-inch (80-cm) circular for magic loop, or DPNs, or two circulars or a 9-inch (23-cm) circular needle.

Important note: *Do check your gauge for fit. Additional sizes can be achieved by going up or down needle sizes.*

Notions

Stitch marker

Scissors

Tapestry needle

Gauge

34 sts x 38 rnds = 4 inches (10 cm) for colorwork.

36 sts x 44 rnds = 4 inches (10 cm) for stockinette and ribbing.

Special Techniques

Knitting Colorwork Socks (page 8)

Making Bobbles (Bigger Version) (page 171)

Kitchener Stitch (page 170)

For all abbreviations, see page 169

The Holly and the Ivy Pattern

Cuff

Cast on 56 (64, 72) sts with CC1 and US 1 (2.25 mm) needle. Divide sts evenly over the two needles and place a marker at the beginning of the round. For DPNs, place half of your sts on one needle and divide the other half over two needles. Join to work in the rnd, being careful not to twist sts.

Ribbing Rnd: *K2, P2; repeat from * to the end of the rnd.

Work Ribbing Rnd for a total of 13 rnds, approximately 1 inch (2.5 cm).

Leg

With CC1 and a US 1.5 (2.5 mm) needle (or needle size to achieve gauge in colorwork), work increase rnd:

Size 1: *K14, M1L; rep from * to the end of the rnd. 4 sts inc'd. 60 sts total.

Size 2: *K8, M1L; rep from * to the end of the rnd. 8 sts inc'd. 72 sts total.

Size 3: *K6, M1L; rep from * to the end of the rnd. 12 sts inc'd. 84 sts total.

Work rnds 1–6 of Colorwork Chart A (page 165), joining MC where shown. The chart repeats 5 (6, 7) times around the sock.

Using MC, and while transferring the sts back onto the smaller needle size, work decrease rnd:

Size 1: *K13, K2tog; rep from * to the end of the rnd. 4 sts dec'd. 56 sts total.

Size 2: *K7, K2tog; rep from * to the end of the rnd. 8 sts dec'd. 64 sts total.

Size 3: *K5, K2tog; rep from * to the end of the rnd. 12 sts dec'd. 72 sts total.

With MC knit 4 rnds.

Garland Section

With MC and US 1.5 (2.5 mm) needle (or needle size to achieve gauge in colorwork), work increase rnd:

Size 1: *K14, M1L; rep from * to the end of rnd. 4 sts inc'd. 60 sts total.

Size 2: *K8, M1L; rep from * to the end of rnd. 8 sts inc'd. 72 sts total.

Size 3: *K6, M1L; rep from * to the end of rnd. 12 sts inc'd. 84 sts total.

Work rnds 1–12 of Colorwork Chart B (page 165), joining CC1 and CC2 where shown. The chart repeats 5 (6, 7) times around the sock.

With MC and smaller needle size, work decrease rnd:

Size 1: *K13, K2tog; rep from * to the end of the rnd, 4 sts dec'd. 56 sts total.

Size 2: *K7, K2tog; rep from * to the end of the rnd. 8 sts dec'd. 64 sts total.

Size 3: *K5, K2tog; rep from * to the end of the rnd. 12 sts dec'd. 72 sts total.

With MC knit 4 rnds.

Rep the Garland Section once more, beginning with the increase rnd.

Short Row Heel

Using CC1, a US 1 (2.25 mm) needle and Needle 1 only, you will now work the heel instructions for your size.

Size 1 only (28 sts on Needle 1):

Row 1 (RS): Sl1, K26, turn work to the WS (leaving 1 st unworked).

Row 2 (WS): Sl1, P25 (leaving 1 st unworked at the end), turn work to the RS.

Row 3: Sl1, K24 (leaving 2 sts unworked at the end), turn work.

Row 4: Sl1, P23 (1 st before the gap), turn work.

Row 5: Sl1, K22 (1 st before the gap), turn work.

Row 6: Sl1, P21 (1 st before the gap), turn work.

Row 7: Sl1, K to 1 st before the gap, turn work.

Row 8: Sl1, P to 1 st before the gap, turn work.

Repeat Rows 7 and 8 five more times.

Row 19: Sl1, K to 1 st before the gap, turn work.

Row 20: Sl1, P7, turn work.

You should have 8 purl sts in the center and 10 unworked sts on each side.

The heel now needs to be worked back and forth, closing the gaps that have been created from turning the work.

Row 21 (RS): Sl1, K6, SSK (working together 1 st on either side of the gap), M1L, picking up under the SSK (do not twist the st). Turn work.

Row 22 (WS): Sl1, P7, P2tog, M1Lp, picking up under the P2tog st (do not twist the st), turn work.

Row 23: Sl1, K8, SSK, M1L, turn work.

Row 24: Sl1, P9, P2tog, M1Lp, turn work.

Continue in established pattern for 14 more rows.

Row 39 (RS): Sl1, K24, K2tog, M1L, turn work.

Row 40 (WS): Sl1, P25, P2tog, M1Lp, turn work.

There are now 28 sts on Needle 1.

Continue to the Foot section (page 164).

Size 2 only (32 sts on Needle 1):

Row 1 (RS): Sl1, K30, turn work to the WS (leaving 1 st unworked).

Row 2 (WS): Sl1, P29 (leaving 1 st unworked at the end), turn work to the RS.

Row 3: Sl1, K28 (leaving 2 sts unworked at the end), turn work.

Row 4: Sl1, P27 (1 st before the gap), turn work.

Row 5: Sl1, K26 (1 st before the gap), turn work.

Row 6: Sl1, P25 (1 st before the gap), turn work.

Row 7: Sl1, K to 1 st before the gap, turn work.

Row 8: Sl1, P to 1 st before the gap, turn work.

Work rows 7 and 8 five more times.

Row 19: Sl1, K to 1 st before the gap, turn work.

Row 20: Sl1, P11, turn work.

You should have 12 purl sts in the center and 10 unworked sts on each side.

The heel now needs to be worked back and forth, closing the gaps that have been created from turning the work.

Row 21 (RS): Sl1, K10, SSK (working together 1 st on either side of the gap), M1L, picking up under the SSK (do not twist the st), turn work.

Row 22 (WS): Sl1, P11, P2tog, M1Lp, picking up under the P2tog st (do not twist the st), turn work.

Row 23: Sl1, K12, SSK, M1L, turn work.

Row 24: Sl1, P13, P2tog, M1Lp, turn work.

Continue in established pattern for 14 more rows.

Row 39 (RS): Sl1, K28, SSK, M1L, turn work.

Row 40 (WS): Sl1, P29, P2tog, M1Lp.

There are now 32 sts on Needle 1.

Continue to the Foot section (page 164).

Size 3 only (36 sts on Needle 1):

Row 1 (RS): Sl1, K34, turn work to the WS (leaving 1 st unworked).

Row 2 (WS): Sl1, P33 (leaving 1 st unworked at the end), turn work to the RS.

Row 3: Sl1, K32 (leaving 2 sts unworked at the end), turn work.

Row 4: Sl1, P31 (1 st before the gap), turn work.

Row 5: Sl1, K30 (1 st before the gap), turn work.

Row 6: Sl1, P29 (1 st before the gap), turn work.

Row 7: Sl1, K to 1 st before the gap, turn work.

Row 8: Sl1, P to 1 st before the gap, turn work.

Work rows 7 and 8 six more times.

Row 21: Sl1, K to 1 st before the gap, turn work.

Row 22: Sl1, P13, turn work.

You should have 14 purl sts in the center and 11 unworked sts on each side.

The heel now needs to be worked back and forth, closing the gaps that have been created from turning the work.

Row 23 (RS): Sl1, K12, SSK (working together 1 st on either side of the gap). M1L, picking up under the SSK (do not twist the st), turn work.

Row 24 (WS): Sl1, P13, P2tog, M1Lp, picking up under the P2tog st (do not twist the st), turn work.

Row 25: Sl1, K14, SSK, M1L, turn work.

Row 26: Sl1, P15, P2tog, M1Lp, turn work.

Continue in established pattern for 16 more rows.

Row 43 (RS): Sl1, K32, SSK, M1L, turn work.

Row 44 (WS): Sl1, P33, P2tog, M1Lp, turn work.

There are now 36 sts on Needle 1.

Foot (All Sizes)

Join back in the round and knit 1 rnd with MC.

Rep the Garland Section twice more, but now following the Foot Colorwork Chart (page 166) for your size in place of Colorwork Chart B. This will instruct you to place bobbles ONLY across the instep. On the second rep, cut CC2 after decrease rnd.

Knit every rnd with MC until you are 2 inches (5 cm) from the desired length of the sock.

With MC and US 1.5 (2.5 mm) needle (or needle size to achieve gauge in colorwork), work increase rnd:

Size 1: *K14, M1L; rep from * to the end of rnd. 4 sts inc'd. 60 sts total.

Size 2: *K8, M1L; rep from * to the end of rnd. 8 sts inc'd. 72 sts total.

Size 3: *K6, M1L, rep from * to the end of rnd. 12 sts inc'd. 84 sts total.

Work rnds 1–5 of Colorwork Chart C (page 165), joining CC1 where shown. The chart repeats 5 (6, 7) times around the sock.

Cut MC.

Toe

With CC1 and US 1 (2.25 mm) needle, work decrease rnd:

Size 1: *K13, K2tog; rep from * to end of rnd. 4 sts dec'd. 56 sts in total.

Size 2: *K7, K2tog; rep from * to end of rnd. 8 sts dec'd. 64 sts in total.

Size 3: *K5, K2tog; rep from * to end of rnd. 12 sts dec'd. 72 sts in total.

Your stitches should now be placed equally on Needles 1 and 2; remove the BOR stitch marker. Needle 1 is holding 28 (32, 36) sts at the bottom of your foot. Needle 2 is holding 28 (32, 36) sts at the top of your foot.

With CC1 and Needle 1, knit 14 (16, 18) sts. Now place the BOR st marker after these sts. This should be in the middle of the sts on Needle 1 at the bottom of your foot.

Setup rnd: Knit 1 more rnd with CC1 to the BOR marker.

Rnd 1 (decrease round):

Needle 1: Knit until 3 sts remain, K2tog, K1.

Needle 2: K1, SSK, knit until 3 sts remain, K2tog, K1.

Needle 1: K1, SSK, knit to BOR stitch marker.

4 sts dec'd.

Rnd 2: Knit all sts.

Repeat rnds 1 and 2 until 20 sts remain on each needle (40 sts in total).

Continue knitting only rnd 1 (dec every rnd) until 10 sts remain on each needle (20 sts in total).

Remove BOR stitch marker. K5 sts to the side of the sock. With 10 sts on each needle, join remaining stitches using Kitchener stitch.

Finishing

Weave in all ends. Soak and block. Repeat instructions for the second sock.

Colorwork Chart A

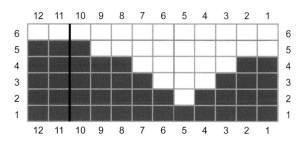

Colorwork Chart B (Garland Section for the Leg)

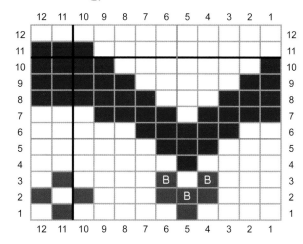

Colorwork Chart C

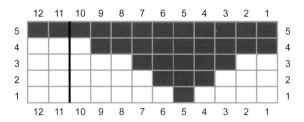

MC: Champagne

CC1: Say Cabernet

CC2: Conifer

B Make Bobble (Say Cabernet)

Foot Colorwork Charts

Size 1

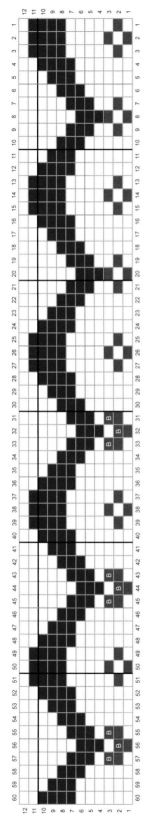

Size 2

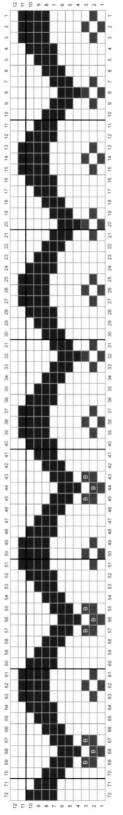

Size 3

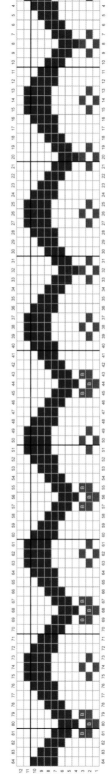

MC: Champagne

CC1: Say Cabernet

CC2: Conifer

B Make Bobble (Say Cabernet)

Yarn Suppliers

I love how colorwork socks are perfect for using scrap leftovers of sock yarn. For many of the patterns in this book, you might need to have only 20 grams or so of yarn for the contrast colors. This makes colorwork socks such a great way to use up any yarn leftovers.

You can knit colorwork socks in any material, from cotton to acrylic to wool (my favorite). Woolier yarns will sit better with colorwork knitting, but yarns with nylon will often wear better and last longer. Yarns mixed with mohair, silk or even nettles are also very durable and strong enough for socks.

As long as they are within the same weight group, you can substitute any sock yarn for the patterns in the book if you find that you are unable to obtain a certain brand, or a colorway is not available wherever you are. I also recommend checking for any leftover sock yarn in your stash for knitting up some of the contrast color details. If you are still able to get the same gauge that the pattern requires, your socks will turn out perfectly.

Below is a list of all the yarn companies and their websites where you can purchase the yarn used in this book.

Countess Ablaze

Important Note: Since the initial writing of this book, Countess Ablaze has stopped producing yarn. See page 64 for information on possible yarn substitutions.

Raindrops on Roses (page 64)

Filcolana

www.filcolana.dk

I Heart Socks (page 151)

Midnight in Zermatt (page 123)

Christmas Eve Skies (page 137)

GigglingGecko Yarns

www.gigglinggeckoyarns.com

Autumn Mice (page 15)

Coffee Break (page 84)

Christmas Eve Skies (page 137)

Dog Walk (page 19)

Midnight in Zermatt (page 123)

Spicy Socks (page 94)

Swan Lake (page 39)

Vitamin C Socks (page 101)

John Arbon Textiles

www.jarbon.com

Forget-Me-Knot (page 51)

Starry Night (page 129)

(continued)

Julie Asselin

www.julie-asselin.com

Happy Poppy (page 57)

Lang Yarns

www.langyarns.com

Gelato Socks (page 89)

Malabrigo Yarn

www.malabrigoyarn.com

I'm Batty for Halloween (page 155)

Neighborhood Fiber Co.

www.neighborhoodfiberco.com

Grape Picking (page 119)

Qing Fibre

www.qingfibre.com

Gelato Socks (page 89)

Raindrops on Roses (page 64)

Retrosaria Rosa Pomar

www.retrosaria.rosapomar.com

Eggs for Easter (page 144)

Rowan Yarns

www.knitrowan.com

Forest Walk (page 113)

Schachenmayr Regia

www.schachenmayr.com

Cherry on Top (page 79)

I Heart Socks (page 151)

Schwedenrot Yarns

www.schwedenrot-yarns.de

Summer Meadows (page 109)

Uschitita

www.uschitita.com

Dog Walk (page 19)

West Yorkshire Spinners

www.wyspinners.com

Counting Sheep (page 25)

Yarn Love

www.yarnloveyarn.com

Blooming Lavender (page 47)

Flutterby Butterfly (page 30)

The Holly and the Ivy (page 161)

Tiptoe Through the Tulips (page 71)

Abbreviations

Here you'll find the list of abbreviations used in the book, to make the patterns easier and faster for you to read.

B = make bobble

BOR = beginning of the round

CC = contrast color(s)

cm = centimeter(s)

dec('d) = decrease(d)

DPN = double-pointed needles

inc('d) = increase(d)

K = knit

K1fb = knit into the front and back of the stitch

K2tog = knit 2 stitches together

Ktbl = knit through the back loop

MC = main color

M1L(p) = Make 1 left. Pick up the bar between the stitch you have just worked and the one you are about to knit (purl), bringing the needle from the front to the back. Then knit (purl) into the back of the stitch, making a new stitch.

mm = millimeter(s)

P = purl

P2tog = purl 2 stitches together

PM = place marker

rep = repeat

rnd = round

RS = right side

Sl1 = slip one stitch purlwise from the left-hand needle to the right-hand needle

SM = slip marker

SSK = slip one stitch knitwise, slip next stitch knitwise, knit the slipped stitches together

st(s) = stitch(es)

WS = wrong side

yo = yarn over

Special Techniques

This section provides further details on more specialized techniques that are used within the patterns to help you complete your socks. If you are still unsure, I recommend having a search on YouTube for any knitting tutorials that might be helpful for you too! I have often done this myself over the years when learning a new knitting technique or skill.

Reading a Chart
(Used in all patterns)

The colorwork charts are worked from right to left, from the bottom to the top. Each pattern will tell you how many times the chart is repeated for each size.

Duplicate Stitch
(Used in Dog Walk [page 19], Swan Lake [page 39] and Eggs for Easter [page 144])

Duplicate stitch is used to imitate knit stitches to add small details to a colorwork pattern. It is similar to adding embroidery onto knitting and creates a matching stitch over a knit stitch. What I find useful with this stitch is that it will add detail without needing to knit more than two or three colors per round.

You will need to first knit the sock without the duplicate stitch details. Then, thread a length of yarn in the color required through a tapestry needle. On the wrong side of your work, near where you want to add your stitches, weave through the back of several stitches to secure the end of the yarn (like weaving in an end).

When you look at your knitting, you will see the fabric of your sock consists of a series of little Vs. Come up through the knitting at the bottom of the V stitch where you would like to work your duplicate stitch. The chart will show you where the stitch should be placed. Slide your needle behind the V that's above the little V stitch that you are covering. Go back down at the bottom of the V in the same space where the needle came up. Try to keep the tension on the yarn tight but not so tight that the stitch cannot be seen. The stitch should be covering the stitch underneath.

If you have never used duplicate stitch before, I recommend using one piece of thread for stitches of each motif. This will result in weaving in more ends, but if you use the same thread for each motif and go round the sock embroidering the stitches, you can often end up changing the tension of the sock and making it difficult to put the sock on your foot.

Kitchener Stitch
(Used in all patterns)

When you are at the end of your sock and ready to use the Kitchener stitch to join the toe stitches together, cut the yarn you have been working with so there is a long piece of thread remaining to sew (or graft) the remaining toe stitches together. With your stitches placed equally on both needles (as described in the pattern), thread your tapestry needle with that long thread of yarn that you have left.

Put your threaded tapestry needle through the first stitch on the front needle knitwise and slip the stitch off the needle.

Now insert your tapestry needle through the next stitch on the front needle purlwise and leave the stitch on the needle.

Pull the yarn through the first stitch on the back needle purlwise and slip the stitch off the needle.

Now insert your tapestry needle through the next stitch on the back needle knitwise and leave it on the needle.

Repeat these 4 steps until you reach the end of the row and you have sewn all stitches together. Then thread the yarn back into the wrong side of the sock and weave in that end. Be sure not to pull the thread too tightly when working the Kitchener stitch. They should resemble knit stitches and almost look like an invisible seam.

Making Bobbles (Smaller Version)
(Used in Autumn Mice [page 15])

Knit in the front, and then the back, and then the front again to make 3 sts in total. Then with your left needle and the stitches on your right, lift st number 2 over st number 3, then st number 1 over st number 3. Now there is one stitch left. Then slip that 1 stitch (without twisting it) back onto your left needle and knit once. Then slip that stitch once again back onto your left needle and knit again. You will now have a nicely shaped bobble at the front of your work.

Making Bobbles (Bigger Version)
(Used in The Holly and the Ivy [page 161])

Knit in the front, and then the back, and then the front and back and front again to make 5 sts in total. Then with your left needle and the stitches on your right, lift st number 4 over st number 5, then st number 3 over st number 5, st number 2 over st number 5, st number 1 over st number 5. Now there is one stitch left. Then slip that 1 stitch (without twisting it) back onto your left needle and knit once. Then slip that stitch once again back onto your left needle and knit again. You will now have a nicely shaped bobble at the front of your work.

Jogless Stripes
(Used in Starry Night [page 129], Flutterby Butterfly [page 30] and Cherry on Top [page 79])

When changing color when working stripes, do not cut the yarn. Carry the unused color up the wrong side of your work. Work the first stitch at the BOR of the second round of the stripe as follows: Pick up the right side of the stitch in the row below the stitch on the needle, put it on the left needle and knit it together with the first stitch on the needle. You will have worked the first stitch of the round twice, but because you work into the stitch below the one on the needle the second time, it will appear that you have only worked it for one round. This will help the jog between the two colors of the stripes disappear, and the beginning of the round for the color change is shifted one stitch to the left.

Whip Stitch
(Used in Forget-Me-Knot [page 51])

Whip stitch is a sewing stitch that sews two pieces of fabric together. (In this case, the cuff of your sock!)

Block your sock (it will be easier to sew the cuff down if the material has been blocked already).

Thread your tapestry needle with the same yarn that you used for your picot cuff.

Arrange the cuff by folding over the fabric evenly so there is a picot edge at the top of the sock.

On the wrong side of your work, insert your needle through the cast-on edge, into the back of a stitch on the fabric underneath (being careful to not go right through the fabric so it is not showing through on the right side of your sock).

Pull the thread back up into the top piece of fabric.

Leaving about a ½-inch (1.5-cm) gap, repeat steps 3 and 4 and continue sewing the two pieces of fabric together, passing in and out of the fabric and circling the cast-on edge as you go around the entire cuff.

Once you have gone round the entire sock, securing the two pieces of fabric together, cut the yarn and sew in the ends.

Acknowledgments

Firstly, a huge thanks to the amazing team of knitters who helped with this book. To my brilliant second sock sample knitter Louise Ling @louling20, to whom I am grateful for her unending motivation, attention to detail and super-speedy sock knitting. And to my fabulous and dedicated test knitting team, who secretly knitted these socks for months and ensured they all fit and that the patterns worked. Firstly, a special thanks to Emily Williams @emilydawnlove, who carefully read and checked every pattern for me. Then to Amy Tucker @amysknottedknits, Deborah Garretty @debgar58, Emmie @emmie.makes, Helena Hurst @edelweiss_knits, Judy Bantli @thegigglinggecko, July Briceno @joyfulyarn, Karin @aarauwestknits, Petra Lang @p_serendipity, Ruth Ogden @craftymamaotter, Sandra @myrthe275 and Tomomi @fioratta. Such a hardworking and talented testing team. Do check out their Instagram profiles for some amazing sock knitting inspiration.

And special thanks to the yarn companies Giggling-Gecko Yarns, Julie Asselin, John Arbon and Yarn Love for contributing yarn for this book. Your yarns and colors were a total inspiration to me.

To Emily Taylor and everyone at Page Street Publishing for giving me the amazing opportunity to write a book about colorwork socks and helping me through this process.

My patient and talented tech editor, Cathy Susko, for working with me for many months on editing these patterns, spotting mistakes and helping these instructions be as understandable and clear as possible.

To my understanding family and ever-encouraging friends for their help and support, providing feedback on my ideas and continuous motivation for me to keep going. Your advice and friendship are invaluable. To photographing guru Toby @tobyjourney (and his dog Kami for inspiring Dog Walk socks!).

A big thank-you to my three fantastic children for allowing me to knit and design socks furiously for many months. To Lola for being the perfect sock model and photographer assistant, and for providing me with many design ideas. To my son Zak for picking up the camera and spontaneously taking my author photo. To my cat Bean for permanently distracting me for food and cuddles, using my knitting needles as toothpicks, chewing on skeins of yarn when I was not looking and for being more popular than me on social media! And to my husband for being full of encouragement for my work and persuading me to take this opportunity while reassuring me that I was completely capable of writing a book on my biggest knitting passion in life, colorwork socks.

And finally, the biggest thank-you to you the knitters, my customers on Ravelry and Etsy, the followers on social media, and the people who I have taught to knit colorwork socks, all who inspire and encourage me every day to continue with my design ideas. I am so grateful for your excitement and support and I love sharing my sock-knitting joy with you!

About the Author

Charlotte Stone is the creator and designer behind Stone Knits and is internationally known for her love of knitting and designing whimsical colorwork knitting patterns, particularly colorwork socks. Her patterns can be found online on Ravelry and Etsy and photos and progress of her work (and life!) on Instagram @stoneknits. Knitting since she was a small child in England with her grandma, she started designing original colorwork patterns in 2017. She has had patterns published in *Laine* magazine and has been teaching colorwork knitting in Zürich, Switzerland since 2019. Charlotte currently lives with her family (and demanding cat Bean!) in the hills above Zürich and is inspired every day by the beautiful Swiss scenery and life.

Index

A

abbreviations, 169

Advent pattern, 161–166

animal patterns, 13–43

    Autumn Mice, 15–18

    Counting Sheep, 25–29

    Dog Walk, 19–24

    Flutterby Butterfly, 30–37

    Swan Lake, 39–43

Autumn Mice, 15–18

B

background color, 11

blocking, 10, 11

Blooming Lavender, 47–50

bobbles, making, 171

butterfly pattern, 30–37

C

Cherry on Top, 79–83

chili pepper pattern, 94–99

Christmas Eve Skies, 137–143

Coffee Break, 84–88

color dominance, 11

colors, choosing, 10

colorwork socks

    animal patterns, 13–43

    care of, 11

    colors for, 10–11

    floats, 10

    flower patterns, 45–75

    food patterns, 77–105

    gauge for, 9

    holiday patterns, 135–166

    mending, 11

    outdoor patterns, 107–133

    sizing, 8–9

    techniques, 8, 170–171

    tips and tricks for, 8–11

    washing, 11

contrast color, 11

Counting Sheep, 25–29

D

Dog Walk, 19–24

duplicate stitch, 170

E

Easter pattern, 144–149

Eggs for Easter, 144–149

F

floats, 10

flower patterns, 45–75

    Blooming Lavender, 47–50

Forget-Me-Knot, 51–56

Happy Poppy, 57–63

Raindrops on Roses, 64–69

Tiptoe Through the Tulips, 71–75

Flutterby Butterfly, 30–37

food patterns, 77–105

Cherry on Top, 79–83

Coffee Break, 84–88

Gelato Socks, 89–93

Spicy Socks, 94–99

Vitamin C socks, 101–105

Forest Walk, 113–117

Forget-Me-Knot, 51–56

G

gauge, 9

Gelato Socks, 89–93

Grape Picking, 119–122

H

Halloween pattern, 155–159

Happy Poppy, 57–63

hole repair, 11

holiday patterns, 135–166

Christmas Eve Skies, 137–143

Eggs for Easter, 144–149

The Holly and the Ivy, 161–166

I Heart Socks, 151–154

I'm Batty for Halloween, 155–159

The Holly and the Ivy, 161–166

I

I Heart Socks, 151–154

I'm Batty for Halloween, 155–159

J

jogless stripes, 171

K

Kitchener stitch, 170–171

knitting techniques, 8, 170–171

L

lavender pattern, 47–50

M

making bobbles, 171

mandarin orange pattern, 101–105

meadow pattern, 109–112

measurements, 8

mending, 11

mice pattern, 15–18

Midnight in Zermatt, 122–127

mountain pattern, 122–127

O

orange pattern, 101–105

outdoor patterns, 107–133

Forest Walk, 113–117

Grape Picking, 119–122

Midnight in Zermatt, 122–127
Starry Night, 129–133
Summer Meadows, 109–112

P

poppy pattern, 57–63

R

Raindrops on Roses, 64–69
reading a chart, 170
rose pattern, 64–69

S

sewing in ends, 11
sheep pattern, 25–29
shoe size charts, 9
sizing, 8–9
Spicy Socks, 94–99
Starry Night, 129–133
stitch
   duplicate, 170
   Kitchener, 170–171
   whip, 171
Summer Meadows, 109–112
Swan Lake, 39–43

T

techniques, 8, 170–171
   duplicate stitch, 170
   jogless stripes, 171

Kitchener stitch, 170–171
   making bobbles, 171
   reading a chart, 170
   whip stitch, 171
tips and tricks, 8–11
Tiptoe Through the Tulips, 71–75
tulip pattern, 71–75

V

Valentine's Day pattern, 151–154
Vitamin C socks, 101–105

W

washing, 11
whip stitch, 171
wool, 11

Y

yarn suppliers, 167–168